By: Kim Edmister

ANNOUNCING...
GOAL OF THE WEEK
GRADES K-5

A Year-Long Guidance Program that Includes Weekly Goals, Daily Announcements and Daily, Teacher-Led, 3-5 Minute Mini-Lessons

This book belongs to Spring Branch Elementary.

© 2014 YouthLight, Inc.
Chapin, SC 29036
All rights reserved.
Permission is given for individuals to reproduce the activities in this book.
Reproduction of any other material is strictly prohibited.
Cover Design by Amy Rule
Layout by Eric Clark
Project Editing by Susan Bowman
ISBN: 978-159850-152-0
Library of Congress Number:
2014930310
Printed in the United States

ACKNOWLEDGEMENTS

First and foremost, I would like to thank Susan Roush, my mentor and friend, who planted the seed for the idea that this finished product represents. I will be forever grateful to you for sharing your magical ways with me, and for the years of collaboration we had creating and implementing a comprehensive character education program to our students in the Corning-Painted Post School District. I will always cherish the years we worked together, and your lasting friendship.

Thank you to the many amazing administrators and teachers I've had the pleasure of working with over the years who have enthusiastically welcomed and supported my efforts to deliver meaningful character education to all students. Thank you for all that you do each day to make a difference in the lives of children. Your dedication and hard work is inspiring!

Thank you to my children and family who have been the sounding board for so many of my ideas over the years. And to my cheerleader in life, my mom - who, since the beginning of time, made me believe that there is nothing I can't do.

DEDICATION

To an amazing teacher - my sister and friend, Tracey. For your undying support and encouragement to complete this project, I lovingly dedicate this book to you.

TABLE OF CONTENTS

INTRODUCTION

WHY THE GOAL OF THE WEEK?

For every educator who has been searching for a way to infuse character education into the school day in a brief, yet meaningful way, look no further! *Goal of the Week* delivers!

Goal of the Week includes:

(10) Monthly character education topics
(40) Weekly goals
(180) Daily mini-lessons to be delivered by classroom teachers to students
(180) Daily "Hey kids!" morning announcement messages

Simple and straightforward, the Goal of the Week mini-lessons are ready made, teacher led discussions that require just 3-5 minutes each day. Absolutely NO prep time is required! It is a powerful, stand-alone, character education program when delivered to individual classrooms, but gains momentum with school wide awareness and implementation! Go one step further by including discussion topics in parent communication (so that meaningful conversations can continue at home) and you've hit a homerun!

Topics include:

MORNING ANNOUNCEMENTS

GOAL: HELP OTHERS FEEL WELCOME

MONDAY: Hey kids! For those of you who are new to our school, WELCOME! For those of you who are returning to our school, WELCOME BACK! If you are a returning student, please look around today and be sure you notice any students who are new to our school! Show your great character today by introducing yourself and offering to be their helper. Your bright smile will help new students feel welcome! Have a great first day back!

TUESDAY: Hey kids! Do you know that smiling at someone is a simple thing to do that lets others know that you are friendly? When you look around today, make sure that you smile at everyone you see. When others see your smile, they will probably smile back – and might even want to be your friend! Smiling is a great way to show your good character and help others feel welcome at the same time!

WEDNESDAY: Hey kids! Have you noticed that no one in our school is exactly like you? We are all different, and that's one of the things that makes our school so special. Show your good character today by respecting the differences of others!

THURSDAY: Hey kids! Make new friends and help others feel welcome by inviting someone new to join you at lunch or recess! Remember that if someone asks YOU if they can sit near you or join you at recess, the answer is always yes! Inviting and allowing others to join you shows your great character and helps others feel welcome!

FRIDAY: Hey kids! Thanks for a great first week of school! Please remember to continue to help others feel welcome at our school. It shows your great character and helps others feel happy to be here with us!

GOAL-OF-THE-WEEK DAILY MINI-LESSONS

WEEK 1
TOPIC: WELCOME (BACK) TO SCHOOL!
GOAL: HELP OTHERS FEEL WELCOME

MONDAY: **Welcome (back) to school!!** Discuss how to introduce yourself to someone new. Remind them to smile. "Hi! My name is _____. What's your name?" (Brainstorm some ideas of what to say next.) "Nice to meet you, _____. (Repeating the person's name will help you remember it.) Learning someone's name is a great first step to making a friend. Talk about what it's like to be new to a school and what each of us can do to help others feel welcome in our school.

TUESDAY: Start each day with a smile! When someone sees you smile, they will think that you are nice and may want to be your friend. When someone smiles at you, be sure you smile back.

Greeting someone is a wonderful way to help others feel welcome. Practice what that sounds like to greet someone in the morning, Good morning (say the person's name if you know it.) Demonstrate the difference between an indifferent greeting, and an enthusiastic greeting.

Good eye contact completes the package. A smile and warm greeting coupled with good eye contact are great ways to start each day! Tell your students that your heart smiles when you are greeted warmly. Take the time to greet each student daily, and notice how they do the same.

WEDNESDAY: Discuss differences. Glasses, braces, how we walk, talk, look – our names. We are ALL different! At our school, we think being different is GREAT! It would be boring if we all were exactly alike. It's not okay to poke fun at or laugh about the ways that we are different. (After all, YOU are different too!) Remind students that teasing is not allowed at our school. Your teacher and the adults at school are here to make sure each and every student feels safe and happy at school. Let them know the procedure for getting adult help when needed.

THURSDAY: Suggest that each student invite someone new to join him or her (at recess, lunch, etc.). It is also appropriate for someone to ask, "May I sit here?" or "May I play with you?" Discuss appropriate responses to those questions… "Sure!" "Yes!" "Certainly!" Make sure that the children know that it would be unkind to refuse.

FRIDAY: Review this week's goal together. Give students an opportunity to share how it went and what worked/didn't work. Allow them to help problem solve together. Remind them that they will need to keep these things in mind any time a new student joins the class.

MORNING ANNOUNCEMENTS

GOAL: BE THE BEST YOU CAN BE!

MONDAY: Hey kids! Coming to school every day is very important to doing well and having a great year! Take some time in the morning to be sure you have everything that you will need for the day! Coming to school every day, on time, with everything you need shows your great character!

TUESDAY: Hey kids! A good night's sleep will help you to be the best you can be at school! Feeling rested helps you to be able to concentrate and work hard during your busy day. Show your great character by getting enough sleep so that you have the energy to be the best you can be at school!

WEDNESDAY: Hey kids! Having a good breakfast helps get your body and brain ready to be your best! Make sure you get up in time to eat in the morning. Your good character shines through when you come to school ready to be and do your best!

THURSDAY: Hey kids! Don't forget to wash your face and hands and brush your teeth and hair before leaving for school. Taking the time to clean up shows that you care about yourself and the people around you!

FRIDAY: Hey kids! It is important to always try your best! Always write in your neatest handwriting and do your best on your school work. Doing your best will make you feel proud and show others your great character!

WEEK 2
TOPIC: WELCOME (BACK) TO SCHOOL!
GOAL: BE THE BEST YOU CAN BE!

MONDAY: Come to school on time and with all of the materials you need for the day. Talk about the importance of coming to school every single day. (Exceptions: gushing blood, throwing up, etc.) Having a mild ache or pain is not good cause to miss school. When you are not in school, you miss important information and we miss you! There are important student jobs for all students and if you are not in school, you cannot do your job.

TUESDAY: Get plenty of sleep. Feeling rested will help prepare you for a great day at school! You will be able to concentrate and do better when you've had a good night's sleep. (Eat a healthy dinner and stay away from soda and sweets so that you are able to sleep.)

WEDNESDAY: Eat a nutritious breakfast. Having something healthy to eat before you come to school (or at school, if you eat breakfast here) gets your body and brain ready to be your best. It can be very challenging to be your best when you are hungry. (Go over nutritious choices.)

THURSDAY: Wash your face and hands and brush your teeth and hair before leaving for school. If you did not have a bath or shower the night before, wash from head to toe with a wash cloth. Wear clean underwear and clean socks and clean clothes.

FRIDAY: We come to school to learn! Some things will be easy for you, and other things may be a little harder. No matter how easy or hard something is, the most important thing is to try your best. Discuss the importance of taking your time on your work so that it is a good representation of your "BEST" work.

MORNING ANNOUNCEMENTS

GOAL: ALWAYS REMEMBER YOUR MANNERS

MONDAY: Hey kids! One way to show your great manners is to say, "thank you" whenever someone does something kind or gives you something. You can show your great character by saying "thank you" in a loud cheerful voice when you go through the lunch line every day.

TUESDAY: Hey kids! Remember your manners when you cough, sneeze or burp! Make sure you turn your head away from others and cover your mouth. Your good character shows through when you use your manners without being reminded.

WEDNESDAY: Hey kids! Show your good manners by helping to keep our bathrooms clean and germ free. Kids with character show their manners by cleaning up after themselves without needing reminders.

THURSDAY: Hey kids! Did you know that it is unkind to laugh when someone makes a mistake? You show great character when you are kind and supportive whenever someone makes a mistake.

FRIDAY: Hey kids! There are lots of ways to show your good manners!

Try these things:
1. When you are lining up, go to the end of the line and stay in your spot.
2. Keep your hands and feet to yourself.
3. Never laugh when someone makes a mistake or behaves inappropriately.

When you remember your good manners, you show your great character!

GOAL-OF-THE-WEEK
DAILY MINI-LESSONS

WEEK 3
TOPIC: WELCOME (BACK) TO SCHOOL
GOAL: ALWAYS REMEMBER YOUR MANNERS

MONDAY: Always say, "thank you" when given something. When someone thanks you, remember to say, "you're welcome" in return. Go over times during the school day when there are opportunities to say, "thank you" (that most kids forget!) Going through the lunch line (to the servers), getting off the bus, getting an ice pack from the nurse, etc. Can you think of more?

TUESDAY: When you cough or sneeze, it is appropriate to turn your head away from others and cover your mouth with the fold of your arm. If you need to burp, your lips should be closed to muffle the sound. (It is never appropriate to laugh!) Afterwards, say "excuse me," with a quiet voice. Never laugh or draw attention to someone else's body noise.

WEDNESDAY: Keep yourself and our bathrooms clean and germ free. Flush the toilet and wash your hands with soap and water after using the restroom. If there are paper towels on the floor, pick them up and put them in the garbage can.

THURSDAY: Everyone makes mistakes. *Everyone!!* Share a story about a time you made a mistake, and others responded in an unsupportive way – laughed at or scolded you. Talk about the feelings you experienced (embarrassment; anger, etc.) Allow students to brainstorm alternate (supportive) responses.

FRIDAY: When it's time to line up, be polite and take your place at the end of the line. Don't race to be first (or next) in line and do not get in front of someone already in line. When walking in line, keep your arms at your sides and walk quietly.

MORNING ANNOUNCEMENTS

GOAL: ALWAYS DO THE RIGHT THING

MONDAY:
Hey kids! Can you "Give me Five?" Hold up one hand, and with your other hand, touch one finger at a time. Say this with me, "Always…Do…The… Right…Thing." Always Do The Right Thing means that you know the rules and you follow the rules. Your good character shines through when you do what is RIGHT even when no one is around to notice or remind you!

TUESDAY:
Hey kids! Can you "Give me Five?" Hold up one hand, and with your other hand, touch one finger at a time. Say this with me, "Always…Do…The… Right…Thing." What do you think is the "right" thing to do when you see someone else making a bad choice? Show your great character by making a good choice even when someone else is not.

WEDNESDAY:
Hey kids! Can you "Give me Five?" Hold up one hand, and with your other hand, touch one finger at a time. Say this with me, "Always…Do… The…Right…Thing." Always Do The Right Thing means that you behave respectfully. Smile. Be friendly. Follow rules. Help others. Your great character shows when you choose to use words that are kind and polite.

THURSDAY:
Hey kids! Hold up one hand, and with your other hand, touch one finger at a time. Say this with me, "Always…Do…The…Right…Thing." Always Do The Right Thing means that when your teacher is out for the day, you follow the rules and behave respectfully for the substitute. You show your good character when you Always Do The Right Thing – even without reminders.

FRIDAY:
Hey kids! "Always…Do…The…Right…Thing" means that you choose to behave responsibly. Remember to show your parents your papers from school, pick up after yourself and keep your promises. When you are responsible, your great character shines through!

GOAL-OF-THE-WEEK DAILY MINI-LESSONS

WEEK 4
TOPIC: WELCOME (BACK) TO SCHOOL!
GOAL: ALWAYS DO THE RIGHT THING

MONDAY: Have kids hold up one hand with all five fingers extended. With the other hand, have them touch each finger one at a time while saying, "Always Do The Right Thing." That's our "Give Me Five" goal. (Allow them to practice several times.) When someone asks you to "Give Me Five" you should proudly hold up your hand and show them our "Give Me Five" goal.

Doing the "right" thing means being responsible by following rules. Talk about rules and laws, and what would happen if no one followed them. Know the rules and follow the rules – even if no one else is around. (Adults will notice, appreciate and respect that you follow the rules. Children who have demonstrated that they know the rules and follow them are often the children who are trusted to do special errands/jobs during the school year.)

Review safety rules that you feel are important to reinforce at this time. It is "right" to know what our rules are and to always follow them.

TUESDAY: Have kids practice the "Give Me Five" goal. When you see someone do something that they shouldn't be doing, **do not laugh**, **do not join in** and **do not copy them**! It's not your job to make sure everyone else follows the rules (that's the grown-up's job). It is your job to follow the rules *yourself*.

WEDNESDAY: Have kids practice the "Give Me Five" goal. Doing what is "right" means being respectful. It is respectful to be kind and polite when you talk. Give examples of polite words and a polite tone of voice. Don't talk back to adults. Discuss what "talking back" sounds like. Give examples… allow children to give examples. Discuss other non-verbal cues that are disrespectful (facial expressions, etc.) Talk about the potential benefits of making respectful choices (avoiding loss of privileges, etc.). When someone makes a reasonable request say, "Sure, I'd be glad to." (It's fun to challenge students to try this at home with parents and report back the response they receive!)

THURSDAY: Have kids practice the "Give Me Five" goal. Talk specifically about "right" choices on the school bus, in the lunchroom and hallway, at recess and when a substitute teacher is visiting. Have children brainstorm what "right" choices look like/do not look like in each instance. Remind students that it is respectful to comply to *reasonable* adult requests at school…even if they are not familiar with who the adult is. (I use a little bit of caution here in the words I choose in my discussions with children around indiscriminately following adult directives, as it has the potential of putting children at risk. Children need help differentiating between *reasonable* and *unreasonable* requests, and empowered to refuse *unreasonable* requests.)

FRIDAY: Have kids practice the "Give Me Five" goal. Doing the "right" thing means being responsible. Remember to show your parents paperwork from school; do your homework; pick up after yourself; keep your word. Discuss other ways for students to demonstrate that they are responsible.

MORNING ANNOUNCEMENTS

GOAL: KNOW WHAT TO DO

MONDAY: Hey kids! Do you know what you'd do if you were ever in a busy place like a store and couldn't spot the adult you were with? When you go home today, talk to the adults in your family about what you should do if that ever happens to you. I like for children to ask someone who works in the store for help. Another option is to ask for help from an adult who has small children with him or her. Look for someone carrying a baby, pushing a stroller, or holding the hand of a small child. Making a plan for what to do if you ever get lost makes those times a lot less scary. "Know what to do" when you are lost!

TUESDAY: Hey kids! It's important to know what to do if there is ever an emergency at home. Do you have a neighbor who might help you? Do you have a phone to call someone? Do you know a phone number to call? Check at home to be sure that important phone numbers are written down and easy to find in case you need them.

WEDNESDAY: Hey kids! Did you know? A stranger is someone that you never saw before. A stranger is someone you don't remember. Strangers can be girls… strangers can be boys. Strangers look just like regular people. And you know what? Almost all of the strangers in the world are good strangers!!

THURSDAY: Hey kids! Do you "know what to do" if you see a gun? Here is a rhyme that will help you to remember what to do. Are you ready? If you see a gun, RUN!! Never touch a gun!! Never pick up a gun!! If you see a gun, RUN!! Guns are dangerous!! Guns can hurt!! If you see a gun, RUN!!

FRIDAY: Hey kids! Do you "know what to do" if you see matches or a lighter? Matches and lighters can make fire and are VERY dangerous. Do NOT pick them up! Do NOT touch them! Knowing what to do when you see matches or a lighter helps everyone stay safe!!

GOAL-OF-THE-WEEK DAILY MINI-LESSONS

WEEK 5
TOPIC: LIFE SAFETY
GOAL: KNOW WHAT TO DO

Message to Teachers: Please use your discretion in your talks with your students. We don't want to cause unnecessary anxiety or worry! Feel free to include the information below in your weekly communication with parents, and encourage them to continue these talks at home with their children.

MONDAY: Unfortunately, many of us have memories of the panic we've felt from being lost. Ask students to raise their hand if they ever were separated from their parents in a public place (store, for example) and didn't know what to do? (Allow students to share, if time allows.) It's important that children have discussions with the adults in their lives so that everyone agrees on what to do in the event that they get separated. I always told my children that if they became lost, they need to stay where they are. I will find them. I didn't want them running around looking for me while I was running around looking for them. Encourage children to have these discussions at home so that they know what their parents want them to do in the event that something like that happens. Encourage children to ask an employee or an adult with children for assistance.

TUESDAY: Many of our young students are left home alone – sometimes in the care of older siblings and other times in charge of younger siblings. It's important that they know where they would go and/or who (two or three choices) they would call in the event of an emergency. What if that line was busy? Go to the next number. Emergency numbers should be placed by the phone. It's important for all students to know their full name and their parents' names.

WEDNESDAY: Ask children, "What does a stranger look like?" (My experience is that most K-5 students will describe variations of mean looking men dressed in black, capes, masks; carrying weapons, etc.) Define for them: A stranger is someone you don't know. ANYONE you don't know. They look like you and me. Tell students that almost every stranger is a nice stranger. They would help you if you needed help. (It is okay to ask a stranger for help if you need it!) BUT, if a stranger is needing help, they need an *adult* helper. Safe strangers don't ask children for help – they ask grown-ups. If a stranger approaches you for any reason, run away! Even if they look really, really nice. Even if they need help finding their cat, or they have candy or toys for you, run away! (Good strangers and bad strangers look the same!) NEVER, EVER go with or get in a car with someone you don't know.

THURSDAY: If you see a gun, RUN! (and tell a grown-up) If it is in a closet, RUN! (and tell a grown-up.) If you see a gun laying on a table or bed or couch, RUN! (and tell a grown-up.) If someone has a gun in their hands, RUN! (and tell a grown-up.) Never stop to look at a gun. Never touch a gun. Never be anywhere there is a gun. Teachers of younger students might want to do a little chant with the kids. Teacher: If you see a gun...Students: RUN! (repeat).

FRIDAY: Talk to children about the importance of NEVER playing with fire. Don't touch matches or lighters. In the event of a fire in your home it's important that everyone leaves the home. Do NOT hide! Do not stop to get dressed or get your favorite toy. Agree on a meeting place outside for family members. Talk to children about what to do if clothing is on fire – never run! STOP, DROP & ROLL. Have students remind parents about changing batteries in smoke detectors.

MORNING ANNOUNCEMENTS

WEEK 6

GOAL: KNOW WHO TO TELL

MONDAY: Hey kids! Do you know who you should talk to if you ever need help? Parents and other family members can be wonderful helpers…but what if they aren't around? Other grown-ups can be wonderful helpers when your parents aren't around. Today's goal is to think about WHO ELSE we could go to if we ever needed help.

TUESDAY: Hey kids! Do you know who the adult in charge is? It is not always the same person. Who is the adult in charge at home? Who is the adult in charge in your classroom? Who is the adult in charge on the bus? Today, think about who the adult in charge is at different times during your day. That way, you will know who to tell if you are needing some help.

WEDNESDAY: Hey kids! Did you know that you have a very important job? That job is to keep yourself safe! If someone is hurting you, your job is to "report" it to the adult in charge. Reporting is something you do if there is danger…or if you feel hurt, worried or afraid. Know who to tell when you have something to "report."

THURSDAY: Hey kids! Did you know that we share an important job of keeping each other safe? If you see or hear someone else being hurt, your job is to "report" it to the adult in charge. Reporting is something you do if there is danger…or if you feel hurt, worried or afraid. Every person has a responsibility to report! It's how we help to keep one another safe!

FRIDAY: Hey kids! Do you know what to do when you REPORT something and it doesn't get better? Your job is to keep reporting!! If you still are feeling hurt, worried or afraid after you report, think about another grown up that you can talk to. Your teacher, (principal's name), (counselor's name) are just a few of the grown-ups that help kids at our school.

GOAL-OF-THE-WEEK DAILY MINI-LESSONS

WEEK 6
TOPIC: LIFE SAFETY
  GOAL: KNOW WHO TO TELL

MONDAY: It's important that children can identify individuals they can turn to for help at any time. Begin discussions this week by having students identify people outside of school that they would turn to for help. Lots of kids will identify their parents, but press them to name additional people (what if their parents are not around?) including other family members, neighbors, parent of a friend, scout leader, coach, teacher, etc.

TUESDAY: Spend some time helping children to identify the "adult in charge" in school and other various locations (library, gym, music, art, lunchroom, recess, school bus, after school care, etc.).

WEDNESDAY: If there is someone at home, on the bus or at school who is hurting your body or repeatedly hurting your feelings, it is important to "report" it to the adult in charge. Reporting is different from tattling. Reporting is something you do if there is danger or you feel hurt, worried or afraid. Every person has a responsibility to report! It's how you keep yourself safe.

THURSDAY: Another job that we have is keeping others safe. One important way that we do that, is by keeping our own bodies safe and in control. Another way that we do that is by watching out for others, and offering to help (or to get help for them) when needed.

FRIDAY: Talk about what to do if you report and things don't get better? Keep reporting. Help identify adults they can turn to when it seems they are not getting the help that they need.

MORNING ANNOUNCEMENTS

GOAL: BE HEALTHY AND SAFE

MONDAY: Hey kids! Did you know that eating healthy food and getting lots of exercise helps to keep your body strong? What kinds of fun activities do you do that help to keep your body healthy and strong? Did you know that too many sreen activities aren't good for your body or your brain? When the weather is nice, make sure you get outside for fresh air, fun and good health! Kids with character do their best to live healthy and safe lives!

TUESDAY Hey kids! Did you know that it's important to get help from a grown up when you need to take medicine? Taking too much medicine or the wrong medicine can make you very, very sick. Show your good character by getting help from an adult anytime you need to take medicine.

WEDNESDAY: Hey kids! Part of being healthy and keeping yourself safe is making sure that you never lick or taste something when you don't know what it is. If you aren't sure if something is safe to eat, check with a grown-up to make sure it's okay. Your great character shows when you check with an adult before you lick, taste or eat something unknown.

THURSDAY: Hey kids! Did you know that playing outside with a friend is not only FUN – but helps you to stay safe? Friends can help us to remember important safety rules when we're outside. They can go for help if someone is hurt. Having a friend with you when you are playing outside is another way to be healthy and safe and show your great character!

FRIDAY: Hey kids! Did you know that a grown up should ALWAYS know where you are and what you are doing? Staying safe means that you always check with a grown up before you go someplace. Knowing what to do to stay healthy and safe is another way to show your great character!

WEEK 7
TOPIC: LIFE SAFETY
GOAL: BE HEALTHY AND SAFE

MONDAY: Exercise is an important part of living a healthy life. Talk about spending time each day participating in an outdoor activity. What do you like to do? Riding bikes, walking, playing kickball, hide and seek, tag, etc. are examples of fun outdoor activities that help you stay healthy. As the weather begins to turn cold, what kinds of things can you do to get exercise? Be sure to limit screen activities as these offer little exercise for your mind and body.

TUESDAY: Only take medicine with adult supervision. Taking the wrong medicine or too much of the right medicine can make you very, very sick. If you don't take enough, it might not help you at all. It's very important that children get help from an adult when needing medicine.

WEDNESDAY: Talk to students about the dangers of eating, licking or tasting anything when they are not sure what it is. They should ask permission from a trusted adult if they are uncertain. Even SMELLING some toxic substances can be hazardous. Tell students that they are responsible for making sure that what they put in their bodies is safe and healthy.

THURSDAY: If/when you are out and about in the neighborhood, make sure that you are with a friend. It's safer to be with others so that if one of you gets hurt, someone else can go for help. Be aware of who is around. Do not go near people or cars you don't know. If a strange car or person approaches you, it's important to leave the area immediately! (Remember that when safe strangers need directions or help, they ask grown-ups – not children!)

FRIDAY: Make sure that the grown-up in charge always knows where you are!! If you ask to go next door, go straight there. If your friend is not home or you change your mind, go back home to tell the grown-up in charge.

MORNING ANNOUNCEMENTS

GOAL: PROMISE NOT TO SMOKE!

MONDAY: Hey kids! Did you know that smoking is bad for your health? When someone smokes, they are breathing in unhealthy chemicals. I have made a promise to never smoke. Your great character shows when you keep your promise to never, ever smoke!

TUESDAY: Hey kids! Did you know that smoking makes your breath, hair and clothes smell like smoke? It makes your teeth and your finger nails turn yellow too! YUCK! I know I'm never going to smoke! Can you say that too? ("I'm never going to smoke!") We make the world a healthier place and show great character when we make a promise to never smoke.

WEDNESDAY: Hey kids! I have a few more reasons why I'm never going to smoke! People who smoke cough more, have more headaches, have more problems with their teeth and can't run as fast as people who don't smoke. I know for sure, I'm never going to smoke! Can you say that with me? ("I'm never going to smoke!")

THURSDAY: Hey kids! Smoking costs lots and lots of money! I don't think it's a good idea to spend money on something that will make me sick. I know I'm never EVER going to smoke. Can you say that with me? ("I'm never EVER going to smoke!)

FRIDAY: Hey kids! Did you know that when your nose can smell the smoke from someone else smoking, it is not healthy for YOUR body? (Repeat that… Did you know that when your nose can smell the smoke from someone else smoking, it is not healthy for YOUR body?) If someone is smoking near you, move away from them if possible. If someone is smoking in the car, ask politely if a window could be rolled down so that you can get some fresh air. Your great character shows when you make a promise NEVER to smoke!

GOAL-OF-THE-WEEK DAILY MINI-LESSONS

WEEK 8
TOPIC: LIFE SAFETY
GOAL: PROMISE NOT TO SMOKE!

MONDAY: Red Ribbon Week is usually held towards the end of October. Although it promotes living a drug free life, I focus my discussions with children around making a promise never to smoke. We do a week of "dress-up" days to celebrate our promise never to smoke. (See the bottom of the page for ideas)

Many of our young students will feel the need to report that various family members smoke. Please stress with children that the focus is *not* on convincing others to stop smoking, but making a promise to never smoke themselves. Once someone starts smoking, it is very, very hard to stop. BE SMART ~ DON'T START!

TUESDAY: We want our students to make a choice for their own lives. Allow them to share "yuck!" stories about smoking. (When I was a little girl, my father would smoke cigars in the car, and I would always get sick!)

WEDNESDAY: Smoking is not healthy. It makes your breath, hair and clothes smell. It makes your teeth and your fingernails turn yellow. People who smoke cough more, have more headaches, have more problems with their teeth and can't run as fast as people who don't smoke. Make a promise to never smoke!

THURSDAY: Smoking costs lots of money! Money spent on smoking is money that can't be spent on other things. If you had extra money, what would you spend it on? Even someone who doesn't smoke very much can spend HUNDREDS of dollars every year!! Heavier smokers might spend THOUSANDS!! Make a promise to never start smoking!!

FRIDAY: Breathing smoke is not healthy for your body. If someone is smoking near you, move away from them if possible. If someone is smoking in the car, ask politely if a window can be rolled down so that you can get some fresh air.

Okay, we've learned that smoking isn't healthy for you; it makes you smell bad, causes health problems, costs lots of money and is very hard to stop once you start. So, why even think about it? Be someone who is proud to make a choice *never* to smoke!

Red Ribbon Week Dress Up Days
Celebrating our healthy, safe and smoke-free lives!
Parents: We appreciate your guidance in helping children make choices that will not distract us from our learning!

MONDAY
Theme: Smoking mixes me up!
What to wear: Clothes inside out and/or backwards

TUESDAY
Theme: Smoking and I Don't Mix
What to wear: Mismatched shoes, socks, clothing

WEDNESDAY
Theme: Put a "cap" on smoking
What to wear: A hat or silly hairdo

THURSDAY
Theme: Follow your dreams; Don't Smoke
What to wear: Pajamas

FRIDAY
Theme: I CAN, You CAN, We CAN – Being smoke free comes in CANS!

What to bring: Non-perishable food items. This day will kick off our holiday food drive. Thank you for your generosity.

MORNING ANNOUNCEMENTS

WEEK 9

GOAL: BE THANKFUL

MONDAY: Hey kids! Did you know that you have so much to be thankful for? Show your great character today by letting someone you care about know how thankful you are for them!

TUESDAY: Hey kids! Saying "thank you" to others is a wonderful way to show your great character and express your appreciation. How many people can you thank today?

WEDNESDAY: Hey kids! Writing a thank you note is a wonderful way to let others know that you appreciate them. Demonstrate your good character by taking the time to send a thank you note to someone.

THURSDAY: Hey kids! There are so many wonderful things about you and about your life! Show your great character by appreciating who you are and the special things you can do!

FRIDAY: Hey kids! Look around today and try to notice all of the wonderful things that you are thankful for. Show your terrific character by appreciating what you do have, rather than wishing for something more.

GOAL-OF-THE-WEEK
DAILY MINI-LESSONS

WEEK 9
TOPIC: THANKFULNESS
GOAL: BE THANKFUL

MONDAY: When discussing thankfulness, often times children will talk about being thankful for "stuff." Focus discussion on non-material items and the things that we take for granted. Get them started and see how many they can come up with. (I am thankful for hearing, seeing, being able to read and write, special talents, having friends, being loved, etc.)

TUESDAY: Challenge students to say "thank you" in a bright and cheerful voice. Show them the difference in how an insincere vs. sincere "thank you" sounds. Practice a sincere, gracious thank you. Brainstorm places in the building they can practice this TODAY. Encourage them to repeat their bright, cheerful "thank you" whenever someone forgets to respond with, "you're welcome." (Maybe they didn't hear you!)

WEDNESDAY: Talk about the importance of writing thank you notes. They are appropriate for acknowledging gifts and/or kind deeds. Talk about what a gracious thank you note sounds like/looks like. (I instruct students to indicate why they are writing, tell how they will use and/or why they like the gift, thank again, sign. Younger children can draw a picture—an adult can assist with a written message. It's also important to use your best hand writing!) Consider incorporating a thank you note into their writing practice.

THURSDAY: Brainstorm things at school that we are thankful for. Look at the list together. Do the people responsible for the things you are thankful for *know* you appreciate their efforts? Encourage the children to verbalize their gratitude.

FRIDAY: Reflect on the week. Does anyone have a story they would like to share about how others responded to the gratitude they expressed? Share a story of your own.

MORNING ANNOUNCEMENTS

GOAL: EXPRESS APPRECIATION

MONDAY: Hey kids! Have you ever heard of The Golden Rule? The Golden Rule is that we treat other people the same way that we like to be treated. Your good character shines through when you follow The Golden Rule and treat others with kindness and respect.

TUESDAY: Hey kids! Take the time to look around and really notice all of the kind things that are going on around you! Show your good character by taking the time today to say "thank you" to someone for their help or kindness!

WEDNESDAY: Hey kids! Stop and notice all of the great things that go on at school today and take the time to compliment at least three people! Your good character shines through when you express your appreciation!

THURSDAY: Hey kids! Wonderful things happen every day at school. Show your good character by taking the time to congratulate someone for their hard work or accomplishment!

FRIDAY: Hey kids! Saying thanks, giving compliments and congratulating others are just a few of the ways we can express appreciation! Show your good character by living a grateful life and expressing your appreciation often!

GOAL-OF-THE-WEEK DAILY MINI-LESSONS

WEEK 10
TOPIC: THANKFULNESS
GOAL: EXPRESS APPRECIATION

MONDAY: Talk about appreciation in relation to the "Golden Rule." (Treat others the way you want to be treated). Doesn't *everyone* like to be acknowledged for the good things they are doing? (Since I like to receive acknowledgement of my good deeds, I will acknowledge the goodness in others.) Talk about what it feels like to be on the receiving end of a compliment.

TUESDAY: Challenge students to begin to **notice** and acknowledge the kindness and good in others. Practice what that sounds like…(Billy, thank you for including me today at recess. Mary, thank you for sharing your crayons with me. David, thank you for helping me when I didn't understand. Mrs. Smith, thank you for planning such a fun art project for us.) As the teacher, go out of your way to model this in an exaggerated way for the kids. (Point out when you are doing it, and even ask the recipient how it felt to hear you say that.)

WEDNESDAY: Talk with the students about giving compliments. We give compliments when we **notice** something that we admire about someone. What are some of the things that we admire? Give examples of what a compliment sounds like. (Try to direct conversation away from material items, and towards intangible items.) "I like the way you draw." "You are really good at math." "You can run really fast!" "You are a nice friend." Challenge them to continue to **notice** and give compliments.

THURSDAY: Talk about congratulating others. Think of instances when a congratulations is in order such as when someone receives (earns) a special recognition (example: earns badges in scouts). Adults say congratulations when someone gets married, has a baby, or gets a new job. How about performing in a play or choral or band concert?

FRIDAY: Allow students to share stories of what they've noticed this week. Who have they complimented and how was that received? How did it feel to receive acknowledgement for their own hard work/kindness? How does it feel to **give** compliments? (Almost as good as receiving them!)

MORNING ANNOUNCEMENTS

GOAL: BE RESPECTFUL

MONDAY: Hey kids! There are millions of ways that you can show respect! Show your great character by focusing on showing respect today and see how many wonderful things happen to you in return!

TUESDAY: Hey kids! Pay special attention to the tone of voice you use when speaking to others. Demonstrate your good character by speaking to others with a respectful tone of voice.

WEDNESDAY: Hey kids! Sit up in your chair, stop fidgeting at your desk and look at the speaker! Demonstrate your good character and respect by being a good listener!

THURSDAY: Hey kids! Show respect by offering to help someone today. Helping others is respectful and it shows your great character!

FRIDAY: Hey kids! Stop yourself before you interrupt someone while they are talking. It takes patience, but it shows respect AND it shows your great character!

GOAL-OF-THE-WEEK DAILY MINI-LESSONS

WEEK 11
TOPIC: THANKFULNESS
   GOAL: BE RESPECTFUL

MONDAY: Talk with students about what respect means – that you care about someone's feelings. To show respect, you use your very best manners. There are lots of different ways to show your respect at school. (See bullets below.) Explain that the best way to ensure that you receive respect is to give it!

- Show respect at school by keeping "your area" (around you) clean in the classroom. Define "your area" and detail what keeping it clean looks like. Allow students to comment on what it's like for them when others don't keep their space clean/neat.

- Show respect at school by pushing in your chair – an easy task that takes minimal effort and contributes to the safety and neat appearance of our school. Discuss places where students can remember to do so.

- Show respect at school by talking and walking quietly in the hallway. Remember that we are here to learn. Respect school rules and the learning of others by walking and talking quietly in our hallways.

- Show respect at school by using appropriate language. Discuss the idea of removing certain words from your vocabulary. (Ex: stupid, shut-up, idiot, etc.) Certainly, vulgar language is never acceptable. Make a choice to NOT repeat the rude words that you hear others say.

TUESDAY: Talk about what a respectful vs. disrespectful tone of voice sounds like. Show the kids what it sounds like. Explain that, aside from being rude, it also conveys a message of, "Go away! I don't care about you!" Encourage children to speak with a respectful tone of voice.

WEDNESDAY: Body language is an important aspect of showing respect. It is respectful to look at the person speaking. Role play what disrespectful body language looks like. Have a student speak to you. While they are speaking; slouch in your chair, look away, play with an object in (or on) your desk. Ask the kids what kinds of messages they receive when you respond that way. Talk about eye rolling and how it is NEVER acceptable, unless someone faints.

THURSDAY: Show respect by holding a door for others, offering to help when someone has their hands full, picking up objects that are dropped. Tell about a time when someone showed you respect by offering to help in these ways. Challenge the kids to see how many times they can show respect this way.

FRIDAY: When two people are talking and you would like to pass by them, it is respectful to walk around – not between them. Please walk around! If there is no room to walk around, then wait quietly and patiently until they are done talking. Saying "excuse me" is appropriate only if there is an emergency and you are unable to wait patiently until the talking stops.

MORNING ANNOUNCEMENTS

GOAL: GIVE THE GIFT OF KINDNESS

MONDAY: Hey kids! Show your great character by giving the gift of kindness to others!

TUESDAY: Hey kids! Something as little as a smile and a pleasant greeting can make someone's day! Give the gift of kindness and show your great character by smiling and greeting others.

WEDNESDAY: Hey kids! Brighten someone's day by surprising them by doing something kind. It will show your great character and make someone's heart smile.

THURSDAY: Hey kids! Give the gift of kindness by remembering your manners wherever you go! Your great character shines through when you remember to say please, thank you, you're welcome, and excuse me!

FRIDAY: Hey kids! The gift of kindness doesn't cost a single penny and it brightens everyone's day! Show your great character by remembering to give the gift of kindness this holiday season!

GOAL-OF-THE-WEEK DAILY MINI-LESSONS

WEEK 12
TOPIC: THANKFULNESS
GOAL: GIVE THE GIFT OF KINDNESS

MONDAY: Kindness is something we all can give. It does not matter how old you are, how smart you are or who you are. We are all capable of being kind. 'Tis the season! Let us give to others the gift of kindness. It doesn't have to take an enormous amount of time and effort and it really can make a difference in someone's day/life! Plus, it feels good! Talk about all the places that children can "Give the Gift of Kindness."

TUESDAY: Talk to the children about smiling and greeting others. Talk about the importance of eye contact and tone of voice. It is not only kind, but also respectful to return a greeting. (For example, when someone says, "Good Morning," it is appropriate to return the greeting with a "Good Morning.") Talk about ways to respond to "Have a nice day!" or "Nice to meet you."

WEDNESDAY: Talk about "just because" kindness…Being kind "just because" it's the right thing to do, it feels good, it brightens someone's day, it makes our school/ families/world better places. Allow children to share times when they were on the receiving end of a random act of kindness. Help children think of age appropriate deeds of kindness they can perform during the upcoming holiday season.

THURSDAY: Being kind means remembering your manners. Re-visit the importance of remembering to say please, thank you, I'm sorry, excuse me and you're welcome.

FRIDAY: Talk about being a gracious gift receiver…what that looks like and sounds like. Mention what you would say if you receive a gift that you do not like. (Find *something* kind to say about it and express appreciation to the gift giver. "Wow, I love the color. Thank you, Aunt Tracey!")

MORNING ANNOUNCEMENTS

GOAL: SAY, "I AM SPECIAL!"

MONDAY: Hey kids! You are special because you are YOU! You are terrific! You matter! And boy, are we glad that you are a part of our school! Show your great character by walking tall and being proud of THE ONE…THE ONLY… YOU!

TUESDAY: Hey kids! Look around a minute and notice all of the ways that people are different. Everyone you see is different. Do you know who else is different? YOU are!!

I am different; I'm not exactly like you or anyone else. You are different; you aren't exactly like me or anyone else. We all are different! And, you'll be happy to know, that's exactly how it is supposed to be!! Our differences make us special.

WEDNESDAY: Hey kids! Did you know that even though some things about us are the same, there are many things that are different. You might have a favorite color, sport, or food that is different from mine. But that's okay! We are all different, and that's the way it's supposed to be. Our differences make us special!

THURSDAY: Hey kids! I am special and you are special – and we are different! There are things that you are really good at, and there are things that I am good at. We might be good at some of the same things, but we also might be good at some different things. I am special because I'm ME. You are special because you are YOU. It's pretty cool that you are the only YOU!

FRIDAY: Hey kids! Even though we are all different; every single person is special. How boring the world would be if we were all exactly the same. Say it loud, say it proud, "I am special!" Are you ready? Say it with me, "I AM SPECIAL!"

WEEK 13
TOPIC: SELF-ESTEEM
GOAL: SAY, "I AM SPECIAL!"

MONDAY: Who you are, how you feel and what you think is important! You are an important part of your family, classroom, school, neighborhood and world! Although there are things that we might have in common, there is no one exactly like you in the world, and there is no one exactly like me. We are all different and special in our own way. We all have value, thoughts, feelings, hopes and dreams. Each one of us has the right to wake up every day and feel good about the person that we are. You are special because YOU are the only YOU! Have kids repeat with you, "I am special!"

TUESDAY: If everyone is different, how do we figure out "the best" way to be? Is it better to be taller or shorter? Is it better to be left handed or right handed? Is it better to be a girl or a boy? The answer is….all of them are the best! You are absolutely perfect just the way you are! You are supposed to be exactly like YOU, and you aren't like anyone else because *you aren't supposed to be!!* And, by the way, *no one else is like you either!!* Have kids repeat with you, "I am special!"

WEDNESDAY: We are all special – we are all different! Allow students to share their favorite food. (Where similarities exist, ask for further details - ice cream flavor, pizza toppings, etc. - to underscore different preferences.) At the end, ask students, "Whose favorite food is the BEST?" (Answer: All of them!) You are special because you are different and you are YOU! You matter! Have kids repeat with you, "I am special!"

THURSDAY: Give students the opportunity to share (through writing, drawing or speaking) a personal attribute. Emphasize that material items (what you have, where you live, etc.) do not establish importance. Encourage them to share examples of kindness, helpfulness, caring for others, sharing, giving, etc. You are special because of the person that you are and all that you can be. You are special because you are you! You matter! Have kids repeat with you, "I am special!"

FRIDAY: Share something (that your students probably don't already know) that you are good at or enjoy doing *outside* of school. Give students an opportunity to do the same. (Perhaps have them turn to a neighbor to share, and then report back something they learned about their classmate.) Point out the variety of responses, and how our differences are what make us unique and special!

MORNING ANNOUNCEMENTS

GOAL: NOTICE SOMEONE'S FEELINGS

MONDAY: Hey kids! Can you tell how someone is feeling just by looking at them? Sometimes we can tell how someone is feeling by the look on someone's face or what their body is doing. Look around today and see if you can name the feeling someone is having just by watching them.

TUESDAY: Hey kids! How have you been doing with noticing the feelings of the people around you? Sometimes it's hard to figure out how someone is feeling just by looking at them. Paying attention and noticing feelings is more important than being able to figure out exactly what someone else is experiencing.

WEDNESDAY: Hey kids! This week we have been working on noticing the feelings of others. Did you know that there is a word for showing that we care about someone's feelings? That word is called EMPATHY. When you show someone that you care about their feelings, you are showing them EMPATHY.

THURSDAY: Hey kids! Have you been practicing showing EMPATHY this week? Remember that EMPATHY is when we show others that we care about their feelings. When we show EMPATHY we are being caring citizens and we are helping to make our world and our school a better place!

FRIDAY: Hey kids! We all like when someone notices our feelings by showing us EMPATHY. It makes us feel important and cared for. BUT, remember…if you are wanting attention ALL the time for your feelings, that can take TOO much work! If you have happy feelings MOST of the time, others will want to help you when you are needing help to feel better.

WEEK 14
TOPIC: SELF-ESTEEM
GOAL: NOTICE SOMEONE'S FEELINGS

MONDAY: Help students learn how to notice the feelings of others. Give non-verbal cues of various feelings and have them guess how you are feeling. Challenge students to notice the nonverbal cues of others to identify how others are feeling.

TUESDAY: Have students try to identify the name of the feeling if the following happened to them…

- You are pulling out your chair to sit down and someone says, "You can't sit there! London is going to sit there!" (Sad, Mad)

- You are walking with your lunch tray over to the table and a friend says, "Sure, you can sit here!" (Happy)

- Someone laughs when you make a mistake. (Embarrassed)

WEDNESDAY Acknowledging someone's feelings means that you do or say something to show them that you noticed what happened and you care. Not every person needs/wants the same thing when they are experiencing an uncomfortable feeling. Sometimes body language can help us to know if someone prefers to be left alone. Others may appreciate having someone say, "Are you okay?" or "Can I help?"

THURSDAY There will be times when someone is feeling one way, and you make a mistake in identifying the feeling. That's okay! The most important thing is that you *notice* and acknowledge another person's feelings. It shows them that they are important to you and that you care. And we all like it when our own feelings are acknowledged and we feel as though others care about us. Tell of a time when someone showed you empathy.

FRIDAY Some teachers might want to take this opportunity to talk about those people who seem to thrive on drama and use exaggerated expressions of their feelings for constant attention from those around them. It can be quite tiresome to have people around you who are in a constant state of turmoil! When that happens, people tend to notice your feelings less and less (because there are always so many of them!) Encourage children to not "cry wolf" when it comes to expressing emotion.

MORNING ANNOUNCEMENTS

GOAL: BE PROUD OF YOURSELF!

MONDAY: Hey kids! Do you know what it means to feel proud? Feeling proud is one of the BEST feelings in the world. It means that you worked hard and are happy with the end result. When you feel proud, you are sort of saying to yourself, "YAY ME!" Parents and teachers LOVE feeling proud of you too! Keep up the great work!

TUESDAY: Hey kids! Being a kid is a lot of work!! Kids have to know the rules, and follow them! Kids have to be their best learners when they come to school every day. Some kids even have jobs to do at home. Did you know that your wonderful CHARACTER shows when you work to do your best in all of your important jobs. You can feel proud of yourself when you work hard to do your best! Keep up the good work!!

WEDNESDAY: Hey kids! It's easy to feel proud of yourself at school when you do your best every single day. Doing your best means that when something is hard, you say "I'll try my best!" Trying your best doesn't mean that you're perfect! Kids with great character try their best each day in school.

THURSDAY: Hey kids! Everyone makes mistakes! Kids with great character tell the truth when they make a mistake and try hard to do better next time. You can feel proud of yourself when you tell the truth about your mistakes!

FRIDAY: Hey kids! Did you know that the BEST days at school are the days that you feel proud of yourself!!? What kinds of things make YOU feel proud of yourself? Try some of those things today and have the best day ever!

GOAL-OF-THE-WEEK DAILY MINI-LESSONS

WEEK 15
TOPIC: SELF-ESTEEM
GOAL: BE PROUD OF YOURSELF!

MONDAY: Feeling proud means that you feel pleased and satisfied about something you did. It means that you worked hard and you are happy with how things turned out. When you feel proud, you are sort of saying to yourself, "Hooray for me!" Feeling proud of yourself is one of the best feelings in the world. Give students an example of a time that YOU felt proud of yourself. Allow students to share their own example.

TUESDAY: Being a kid isn't always easy! You've got the very important job of coming to school every day and doing your best, being a kind friend to others, remembering and obeying the rules, taking care of your body (brushing, cleaning, combing, etc.), helping out at home and at school! Some of you also have "extra" things to keep track of—sports, scouts, lessons, etc. Take a moment to allow children to share some of the different responsibilities they have. Ask them, "How are you doing with all that is going on in your life? Are you doing your best?" Have students reach around and give themselves a pat on the back! It takes a lot of work to be a kid and do all the things you do! You can feel proud of all that you do!

WEDNESDAY: One way to feel proud of yourself is to do your best work. When you try your best, the results are usually positive. Even when something is hard or you are not particularly good at something, trying your best means that you give it your all. Be proud of being and doing your best! That's all anyone can ask of you!

THURSDAY: Nobody's perfect! (Don't expect that you will be!) We all make mistakes. Be proud that you try really hard to make good decisions and that you accept responsibility for your actions when you make mistakes. Be proud of your honesty and your attempts to make things better once you've made a mistake. That's very hard for some people, and something to be really proud of!

FRIDAY: When you make choices that you feel proud of, you have a great day! Review important choices at school that ensure a great day at school. (Example: following the rules, doing your best, being kind, including others, etc.)

MORNING ANNOUNCEMENTS

WEEK 16

GOAL: OFFER TO HELP

MONDAY: Hey kids! Is there someone you can offer to help at school this week? Maybe you could hold open a door or do a special job for your teacher. Maybe you could offer to help a friend with something they are having trouble with. Kids with great character find many different ways to be helpers at school!

TUESDAY: Hey kids! It's a busy time of year and your help is needed at home too! There are lots of different ways that you can be a helper at home. Can you think of some? You can clean up your room, pick up your toys and even ask to help with a special job. Grown-ups LOVE having extra helpers, and kids with great character are really good at giving extra help when it's needed.

WEDNESDAY: Hey kids! Did you know that your help is also needed around your neighborhood? Kids with great character make sure that they clean up their outdoor toys and trash, and even pick up extra trash that they see laying around. Offering to help shovel snow or rake leaves are other wonderful ways for kids to help in the neighborhood. Your great character shows when you help to keep your neighborhood clean!

THURSDAY: Hey kids! We are so THANKFUL when someone offers to help us out when we are in need. Who has been a good helper to you lately? Make sure you give an extra special "thank you" to the wonderful people who offer to help you at school and home.

FRIDAY: Hey kids! Did you notice? Helping at school, home and our neighborhoods makes US feel proud of ourselves. Kids with great character offer to help whenever help is needed. You should feel proud of all the wonderful ways that you offer to help others. Keep up the great work!

© YouthLight

GOAL-OF-THE-WEEK DAILY MINI-LESSONS

WEEK 16
TOPIC: SELF-ESTEEM
  GOAL: OFFER TO HELP

MONDAY: Remind students to continue to "Give the Gift of Kindness" this holiday season. Each and every one of us has a lot to offer and we can all make a difference in our own lives and the lives of others.

Brainstorm ways that children can offer help to others at school. How can you help in the classroom/related arts/café/hallways? Remind them that by following our school rules, they are helping by allowing others to be and do their best. Offering to help is KIND! Talk about the "ripple" that occurs when kindness is given. Challenge the kids to make deliberate attempts to offer help this week.

TUESDAY: Brainstorm ways that children can offer to help at home. How can they help parents and siblings? (Cleaning up after themselves, helping younger siblings, performing simple household chores like taking out the trash, caring for animals, etc.) What about helping other family members, like grandparents? Challenge students to be extra helpful at home this week.

WEDNESDAY: Brainstorm ways that children can help around their neighborhoods: picking up litter, keeping track of their bikes and toys, making safe choices, sweeping the walkway, shoveling a neighbor's driveway, etc.

THURSDAY: Give an example or two of someone offering to help you during the week. Tell them how you felt about receiving the help - thankful, relieved, happy, etc. Allow the children time to talk about instances where others offered help to them this week.

FRIDAY: Allow the children time to share what they have done this week to offer help to others. Challenge them to continue to give the gift of kindness by offering to help at home and at school.

MORNING ANNOUNCEMENTS

GOAL: THINK OF HOW THE OTHER PERSON FEELS

MONDAY: Hey kids! I hope you all have enjoyed your break. If you receive a gift that you are especially excited about, think about how someone else might feel who didn't get something that they had hoped for. It's wonderful to feel excited and thankful for the gifts we receive, but your great character shines through when you think about how others might feel, before you speak.

TUESDAY: Hey kids! It's important to know how to whisper when you are somewhere that you need to be quiet; but whispering to one friend in front of other people makes almost everyone feel bad! If you have private information to share, it's always best to do it when others aren't around, so that no one feels left out by your whispering.

WEDNESDAY: Hey kids! Do you know what a "put-up" is? It is saying something nice to someone. It's a compliment. It usually makes others smile and it always makes them feel wonderful! Show your kindness and great character every day by giving "put-ups" to others.

THURSDAY: Hey kids! Have you ever heard of The Golden Rule? The Golden Rule says that we should treat others the way we would like others to treat us! Doesn't that sound like a wonderful idea!!?? Make sure you show your great character by thinking about other people and making sure that you are always treating them with kindness and respect.

FRIDAY: Hey kids! Have you ever felt left out or lonely?? Look around and notice others who might be feeling left out and invite them to join you! Including others shows your great character and also shows them that you care about their feelings.

GOAL-OF-THE-WEEK DAILY MINI-LESSONS

WEEK 17
TOPIC: EMPATHY
  GOAL: THINK OF HOW THE OTHER PERSON FEELS

MONDAY: The most important things in life are not THINGS! Talk to children about how it feels when someone brags (about a gift they received, a trip or birthday party.) Say to children, "Pretend that I've been wanting a new bike for a very, very long time. If someone came to school and said (in a bragging voice), "I got a brand new bike!" – how do you think I would feel? (Allow children to respond.) Tell children that bragging about gifts, trips or parties can hurt the feelings of others and is not polite.

TUESDAY: Talk about whispering and places where whispering is appropriate, or even preferred (such as church, library, hospitals). Then discuss how it feels and what you think when someone whispers in front of you. ("They **must** be talking about *me*!") Encourage students to share private information away from others so that feelings aren't hurt. (Specifically mention whispering during lunch and recess, as these are the times when it happens the most.)

WEDNESDAY: Introduce the idea of "put-ups." They are the encouraging, kind and supportive words we say to one another. They are the things we say that "lift" others UP. "Put-ups" are the opposite of put-downs. Brainstorm put-ups. Talk about what it feels like to receive a put-up. Encourage students to practice giving put-ups.

THURSDAY: Talk about The Golden Rule. Don't make comments about what someone looks like, what they are wearing, their grades, etc. "If you don't have something nice to say, don't say anything at all." Share a personal account of a time when you felt bad about something someone said to you or about you. Tell the students how you felt when that happened. Reinforce the idea that every single person has the right to feel good about coming to school!

FRIDAY: Talk about what it feels like to be left out. Encourage students to look around – specifically during lunch and recess – and notice who might need to be included. Talk about how unselfish and kind it is to include others. Discuss that when someone asks to be included, it is unkind to refuse.

MORNING ANNOUNCEMENTS

GOAL: BE A GOOD LISTENER

MONDAY: Hey kids! Being a good listener is an important part of being a good student and a good friend. Looking at the speaker when they are talking to you is respectful and shows your great character.

TUESDAY: Hey kids! When someone is talking to you, make sure you look with your eyes AND STAY STILL! Looking at the speaker and keeping your hands, feet and body still is such a respectful way to listen to someone and shows your great character.

WEDNESDAY: Hey kids! We know that respectful listeners look with their eyes, keep their bodies still...and do you know what else they do?? They THINK about what the person is saying. Show that you are a respectful listener by remembering these three important steps: LOOK, STAY STILL, THINK.

THURSDAY: Hey kids! Did you know that good listeners don't interrupt? Unless it's an emergency, do NOT interrupt when someone is talking to you...and do NOT interrupt even when someone is talking to someone else. Waiting for others to finish talking shows respect and demonstrates your great character.

FRIDAY: Hey kids! When grown-ups speak to us at home and school, sometimes we have questions. If you have a question, make sure you wait until the adult is done talking...and then ask your question. At school, we raise our hands and wait to be called on. Remember to show your great character by remembering all of the important steps to being a good listener.

GOAL-OF-THE-WEEK DAILY MINI-LESSONS

WEEK 18
TOPIC: EMPATHY
GOAL: BE A GOOD LISTENER

MONDAY: Making eye contact with the person speaking is the first step to being a good listener. It sends a message to the speaker that, "You are important to me and I care about what you have to say." Demonstrate for students how to turn their bodies towards (facing) the speaker – as opposed to facing away from and turning their heads to look.

TUESDAY: Step two to being a good listener is, STAY STILL! Keep your hands, feet and body still. Give an exaggerated demonstration of what it looks like to be talking to someone who is in perpetual motion. Ask the children how it feels when THEY are talking and the (intended) listener's hands, feet and/or body are distracting? Even subtle movement (for example playing with a shoelace or wiggling a loose tooth) sends the message that you are not focusing on the speaker.

WEDNESDAY: Step three to being a good listener is THINK! Think about what the person is saying. Focus on the meaning of their words and the message they are trying to convey. Repeat the words you are hearing silently in your mind. Thinking about what the speaker is saying will help your brain to remember what is said, and help you to be your best learner.

THURSDAY: Don't interrupt! Unless danger is looming, allow others to complete what they are saying without interruptions. Do not interrupt when someone is talking directly to you, and do not interrupt when someone is talking to someone else. (This includes phone conversations!) This means that you wait patiently nearby until the talking has stopped. Instruct children to use "excuse me" in emergency situations **only** – when personal well-being and/or safety are in jeopardy.

FRIDAY: Often times when a speaker has finished talking, they will ask if there are any questions? If they don't ask and you have a question, feel free to ask. In the classroom setting, raise your hand and wait to be called on. Review the steps to being a good listener: LOOK, STAY STILL, THINK! Encourage students to practice being a good listener at home and at school.

MORNING ANNOUNCEMENTS

GOAL: APPRECIATE DIFFERENCES

MONDAY: Hey kids! Did you know that, even though we look very different on the outside, there are lots of ways that people all over the world are the SAME? How many can YOU think of? I know that every single person in the world has a heart and feelings, just like you and I do. Every single person wants to have friends, wants to be liked and wants to be included when you are talking or playing. Your good character shines through when you remember, (even though we look very different on the outside) we all are the same on the inside.

TUESDAY: Hey kids! People are different in lots of different ways. I know that I'm sure glad that we're not all the same! Have you ever noticed how different YOU are? You might be taller or shorter than other kids, your hair, eyes or skin might be a different color, and you might have a talent that someone else doesn't have. There are a million things about you that are different from other people, and all of those things sure do make you special! Feeling proud of the many wonderful ways that you are different helps your good character to shine through!

WEDNESDAY: Hey kids! Have you ever noticed that different people are good at different things? Having different strengths and talents is a wonderful thing, because then there are people to do all the different jobs in the world. If we ALL were good at being doctors, there wouldn't be anyone left to do all the other jobs. I'm really glad we live in a world where different people are good at different things. That way, YOU can do the jobs that YOU like to do, and I can do the jobs that I like to do, and together we can work to make the world a better place.

THURSDAY: Hey kids! Our goal today is to think about some of the many things that YOU are good at! Every person contributes to make our world a better place. What are some of the special skills and talents that you have that make you different and special?

FRIDAY: Hey kids! Look around and notice the special skills and talents of the people around you. When you notice something that someone is good at, and then give a compliment to someone, you are showing that you appreciate the many ways that we are different AND your great character shines through!

GOAL-OF-THE-WEEK DAILY MINI-LESSONS

WEEK 19
TOPIC: EMPATHY
GOAL: APPRECIATE DIFFERENCES

MONDAY: Talk for a few minutes about the ways that we are the *same.* (We all have a heart, feelings, want to be liked, have friends, be accepted be appreciated, don't want to be teased, etc.) Show respect to others by respecting the feelings of others.

TUESDAY: Respect differences first by acknowledging and appreciating that we are all different. (Ask students to think of *themselves.* In what ways are *you* different?) Brainstorm all the ways that we are different. YOU are different! Never, ever, ever point out or make fun of ways that others are different. (Ex: hair color, clothing, grades, athletic abilities, etc.) Be most proud of the things about YOU that make you different!

WEDNESDAY: Show respect by acknowledging and appreciating that everyone is good at *something.* If everyone was good at the same thing, we wouldn't have people to fill all the jobs of the world. Think about it. If *everyone* was great at baseball, we would have too many baseball players and no one left to be doctors, teachers, veterinarians. How would the world survive?

THURSDAY: Ask students to share a strength that they have. Start by sharing one or two of your own. For example, "I'm good at baking and reading." Allow students to share a personal strength or two. End by reinforcing, "Isn't it great that we all are good at different things?"

FRIDAY: Ask students to acknowledge the strengths of others by paying a compliment. "I really like your hand writing." "Wow, you sure can run fast!" Allow a few minutes for several students to share strengths they've noticed/admired in others. (Teachers are encouraged to start this activity by paying a compliment to someone who might not be recognized by a classmate.) Once a person has been complimented, encourage children to compliment someone different. Solicit from 5 or 6 students. Don't solicit from so many that it becomes obvious that some children are not recognized.

MORNING ANNOUNCEMENTS

GOAL: SHARE

MONDAY: Hey kids! Most of the time, sharing is a very kind thing to do. But sometimes...sharing isn't healthy...and can even be dangerous! Remember that at school, we don't share food of any kind. Did you also know that it's never a good idea to share drinks, chapstick or combs either? When we remember these things, we help to keep each other safe and healthy.

TUESDAY: Hey kids! There are lots of things at school that we use that really don't belong to us at all! Even though we get to use desks, chairs, computers and supplies, they don't actually belong to us. They belong to the school. Your great character shows when you graciously share property that belongs to the school.

WEDNESDAY: Hey kids! Did you know that sharing means sometimes you have to play what someone else wants to play. You don't have to always have your own way! It's better to take turns deciding what to play! Sharing the decision about what to play shows cooperation AND your great character.

THURSDAY: Hey kids! Did you know that there is just ONE person in the world you are in charge of? That's YOU. That means that you are the BOSS of you, and only YOU. Sharing friends at home and school is another great way for you to show your good character.

FRIDAY: Hey kids! When you are sharing the "last" of something at home (like the last cookie or piece of pizza), make sure you let the other person choose which half they would like to take. Sharing shows your good character and it's polite to allow the other person to choose which half they would like.

GOAL-OF-THE-WEEK DAILY MINI-LESSONS

WEEK 20
TOPIC: EMPATHY
GOAL: SHARE

MONDAY: Talk about times (and items) when it is appropriate to share (and not share) at school. (Don't share food, combs, chapstick, test answers.) Reinforce reasons for school rules about sharing (not sharing) these things.

Despite the fact that sharing is kind, talk to students about respecting others when they choose not to share their items. If you have a friend that has difficulty sharing, you can model what sharing looks like/sounds like. In addition, if *you* have an item that is particularly hard to share, it is kind to choose not to play with it in front of others.

TUESDAY: Identify community items that we have to share at school. (Desks, chairs, school supplies, carpet etc.) Remind students that although they may have areas/items designated for their personal use, they do not necessarily own these things. Discuss how to politely navigate situations at school when someone might be using something that you perceive to be "yours." (For example, someone is sitting in your seat/spot.)

WEDNESDAY: Sharing means that sometimes you have to play what the others want to play and think about them first. You don't always have to have your own way! Talk to students about compromise when deciding what to play during recess.

THURSDAY: Talk to students about including others and remind them that "sharing" friends is kind. Intermediate teachers could discuss the notion of "taking away" friends. (Everyone is their own boss...no one student is "in charge" of another.) Talk to kids about how it is unkind to say, "If you are going to be friends with her, you aren't my friend anymore." We all can and should be friends.

FRIDAY: When splitting the "last" of something with someone else, explain that it is kind if the person who is doing the dividing allow the other person to pick which half they will take. For example, when (at home) splitting the last cookie with a sibling, you should allow your brother/sister to choose which half they will take. (If you want to do the picking, you should allow the other person to do the splitting!)

MORNING ANNOUNCEMENTS

GOAL: BE HONEST

MONDAY: Hey kids! Our goal this week is to be honest. Did you know that being honest and telling the truth is the same thing? Telling the truth is important ALWAYS! Make sure that when you go to the movies, out to dinner or to a fun park, you tell the truth about your age. Telling the truth is definitely an important part of your good character!

TUESDAY: Hey kids! This week we're talking about the importance of honesty. Have you ever been in the store to buy something and been given too much money back? Your good character shows when you tell the truth about getting too much money from someone by mistake.

WEDNESDAY: Hey kids! Did you know that you are being honest when you find something that doesn't belong to you and you try your best to give it back to the person who lost it? Finding something that isn't yours does NOT mean that you get to keep it! Kids with great character are honest and work hard to return things that they find.

THURSDAY: Hey kids! Being honest means that when you tell someone that you will do something, you do your very best to keep your word. That means that you do what you say you will do. Keeping your promises is another way to be honest and show your great character!

FRIDAY: Hey kids! Our goal this week has been, Be Honest. Telling the truth about your age, giving back money when you are given too much change, returning things that you find and keeping your promises are all ways that you show that being honest is an important part of your good character.

GOAL-OF-THE-WEEK DAILY MINI-LESSONS

WEEK 21
TOPIC: TRUTH/COURAGE
GOAL: BE HONEST

There are so many opportunities for children (and adults) to practice being honest. Each day teachers can tell a story of a time when they either told the truth or appreciated the honesty of someone else.

MONDAY: Sometimes restaurants, movie theatres and amusement parks set their prices based on a child's age. Telling someone you are younger than you are can mean that you pay less money. Telling someone that you are older than you are might mean that you are allowed to do something you are not old enough to do. For your safety and for the sake of "doing the right thing," when someone asks you how old you are, be honest!

TUESDAY: When we go to the store to buy something, sometimes we get change back from the sales clerk. Every once in awhile, the sales clerk makes a mistake and gives us too much money back. When that happens, the sales clerk may get in trouble from his/her boss. Sometimes they are made to replace the money that is missing from their cash register, and sometimes they even lose their job! It's the "right thing to do" to be honest when someone gives you too much change by accident.

WEDNESDAY: Any time you find something that doesn't belong to you that means that somebody lost it! When you find something, it is not yours to keep! (Keeping something that doesn't belong to you is called **stealing!)** Do your best to "turn in" anything that you find, so that it can be returned to the person who lost it. (Discuss where to go to turn in "found" items at school.) It is the "right" thing to do when you are honest and turn in items that you find. (Just think about how happy you will feel when you lose something special and you get it back because the person who found it turned it in instead of keeping it!)

THURSDAY: It's important that people believe you when you say something. Make sure that when you say you will do something, you do your very best to do it. It's important to be honest by keeping your word/promises. If you say, "I will play with you at recess" – do what you have said you would do. Be careful not to make promises that you might not be able to keep. It's important that others can believe you.

FRIDAY: Share a story of a time when someone was honest with you and you appreciated it, or someone was dishonest and you were disappointed. Point out that when someone does not keep their word, it becomes harder to believe them the next time they make a promise. Allow students to share feelings when someone did not keep their word and/or times when they appreciated the honesty of others.

MORNING ANNOUNCEMENTS

GOAL: HAVE THE COURAGE TO TRY...AND TRY AGAIN

MONDAY: Hey kids! Trying something new can be a little bit scary, but it sure can be fun! Do you have the courage to try something new? Try sitting next to someone different during lunch today, or playing with some different kids during recess. Trying something new shows your enthusiasm, curiosity and great character!

TUESDAY: Hey kids! Can you remember a time when something was hard for you, but you had the courage to keep on trying? Most of you have already shown courage when you were learning how to tie your shoe, learning to ride a bike, or even trying to pull a tooth! You demonstrate courage when you remain calm and keep on trying when something new is challenging for you.

WEDNESDAY: Hey kids with courage have a "Never Give Up" attitude. If something is hard, they try harder!   Show your great character today by TRYING...and then TRY, TRY, AGAIN! You might be surprised by all the wonderful things you are able to do!

THURSDAY: Hey kids! This week, our goal is about having the courage to TRY. But, let's face it. Sometimes things are just really challenging for us. When you have the courage to TRY and TRY and TRY, and STILL can't do something...that shows REAL courage! You will find that MOST of the time, you WILL be able to do things that you never thought were possible.

FRIDAY: Hey kids! Kids with courage say these words to themselves, "I think I can, I think I can." When something is extra hard for you, take a deep breath and say, "I think I can, I think I can." When you have the courage to keep on trying, guess what you just might find out?? You just might find out that YOU CAN!

GOAL-OF-THE-WEEK DAILY MINI-LESSONS

WEEK 22
TOPIC: TRUTH/COURAGE
GOAL: HAVE THE COURAGE TO TRY...AND TRY AGAIN

MONDAY: Share a story with your class about a positive outcome when you had the courage to try something new. Challenge students to try *something* new this week. Give them some ideas: Sit with someone new at lunch, try a different activity at recess, come up with a new and improved homework routine, challenge yourself to argue less with siblings/parents/classmates. Tell them you will be asking them on FRIDAY about how it went. For younger students, make a mental note of examples to share with the group on FRIDAY.

TUESDAY: Let the students share stories of times when *they* have had the courage to keep on trying. For your younger students, ask who has had the courage to practice how to tie, read, ride a two-wheeler, have a tooth pulled? For older students, ask who has had the courage to tell the truth, be the "new kid" at a new school, be a good sport when you lost at something, be kind to someone who has not been kind to you? Challenge the kids to notice acts of courage and report back about their observations.

WEDNESDAY: **The greatest courage often follows failure. . . having the courage to try AGAIN.** Refer to the story of *The Little Engine that Could* (or some other story of perseverance that the students might be familiar with.) What would have happened if he said to himself, "There is no way I can do this – This is too hard?" Great things happen for those who have a "try, try again" attitude. Relate this to a student you have known in the past. Tell a story of a time when you persevered when "the going got tough."

THURSDAY: No one is successful ALL of the time. No one is good at every single thing in life. Some things come easy to you and other things are more difficult. Give students an example of something that is easy/hard for you. Ask students, "What is something that is easy/difficult for you?" The difference between people who do great things in life – and those who don't – is determination; a spirit that keeps on trying.

FRIDAY: Talk to students about their internal dialogue – what they say to themselves when something is difficult for them. Saying things like, "This is too hard." "I can't do this." "I'm never going to get this" - are all self-defeating. Encourage students to change how they talk to themselves about their failures – "At least I tried." "I can always try again." "It didn't work so well. Maybe I can get some help the next time." "I'm proud of myself for trying." "It would be easy to give up, but I'm going to try again."

MORNING ANNOUNCEMENTS

WEEK 23

GOAL: ADMIT A MISTAKE

MONDAY: Hey kids! Did you know that EVERYONE makes mistakes? That's right! Making mistakes is just part of life. Your great character shines through when you tell the truth and work hard to fix your mistakes.

TUESDAY: Hey kids! Do you remember that EVERYONE makes mistakes? Make sure you remember to take the time to say that you are sorry. Kids with great character do their best to make things better when they make mistakes.

WEDNESDAY: Hey kids! Mistakes happen to EVERYONE. Another way to show someone you are sorry is to do something for them to demonstrate your regret. Kids with great character use their words and sometimes also do something to someone show they are sorry.

THURSDAY: Hey kids! Do you know the words to say when a grown up asks you about a mistake you've made? We show our great character when we tell the truth and say, "I did it and I'm sorry" when someone asks us about a mistake we made.

FRIDAY: Hey kids! Remember that EVERYONE makes mistakes once in awhile. When you tell the truth about your mistakes, say you're sorry with your words or an "I'm sorry" letter, and try your best not to make the same mistakes over and over, you are showing great character!

GOAL-OF-THE-WEEK
DAILY MINI-LESSONS

WEEK 23
TOPIC: TRUTH/COURAGE
   GOAL: ADMIT A MISTAKE

MONDAY: Admitting a mistake can take courage. (We worry about "getting into trouble.") However, without exception, EVERYONE makes mistakes! Talk to students about how they are not expected to be perfect. However, they are expected to be honest about their mistakes and to work hard to correct them. (That means that they are not making the same mistakes over and over and over.) Give students an example of a recent mistake you made, and what you did to make things better.

TUESDAY: When you make a mistake that impacts others, it is appropriate to apologize. Go over the steps to making an apology.

1.) Look the person in the eye.
2.) Say, "I'm sorry for (say what happened)."
3.) Say, "The next time I will..." (make sure this is phrased in terms of what they WILL do instead of what they will NOT do.)
4.) Say, "Do you forgive me?"

The person who is receiving the apology can reply by saying,

1.) "You're forgiven." or "I forgive you."
2.) "Thank you for apologizing."

If time permits – allow the children to role play this.

WEDNESDAY: When you have made a mistake, an apology of words is a wonderful place to start. But, you aren't finished! It's important to also *show* the person you are sorry by taking an action step. You need to think of something helpful that you could do for the person that will *show* them that you are sorry for your mistake. Is there something you could do to help them, or show them that you want to be their friend? Help students brainstorm appropriate action steps to show someone that you are sorry for your mistake.

THURSDAY: Introduce/Practice the steps to approaching an adult about a mistake you have made:

1.) Say, "I know it's important to tell the truth, right?"
2.) Tell the story of what happened.
3.) Say, "I'm really sorry."
4.) Say, "Do you forgive me?" or, "Can you help me…(clean up)?"

FRIDAY: Allow students the opportunity to share mistakes they have made during the week, and how they had the courage to admit their mistakes. Share a story of your own.

MORNING ANNOUNCEMENTS

GOAL: STAND UP FOR WHAT IS RIGHT

MONDAY: Hey kids! Do you know what, "Stand up for what is right" means? It means that when you see or hear something that hurts another person, you have the courage to say or do something. If someone is making a bad choice, standing up for what is right means that you don't copy the bad choice. Standing up for what is right sometimes takes courage, but that's what kids with character do!

TUESDAY: Hey kids! Have you ever seen or heard someone being mean to another person? When that happens, what do you do? "Standing up for what is right" means that we say something or do something to help when something bad is happening. When you say, "Please don't be mean to my friend," that is standing up for what is right. Your great character shows when you stand up for what is right!

WEDNESDAY: Hey kids! Did you know that there is a difference between being bossy and standing up for what is right? Someone who is bossy likes to be in charge of everyone else, and they usually aren't very kind about it. Most people don't like being bossed around one bit! Standing up for what is right is a helpful and caring thing to do, and people are always thankful for your help! It's important to know the difference between being bossy and standing up for what is right. If you are needing extra help to understand the difference, be sure you ask a grown up.

THURSDAY: Hey kids! Did you know that standing up for what is right means that you tell the truth even when you might be worried to do that? Being honest is always the "right thing" to do. It shows your great character AND it shows that you believe in Standing Up for What is Right.

FRIDAY: Hey kids! We've been talking about Standing Up for What is Right this week. If you are ever confused about what to do, be sure to ask a trusted grown-up for some help. There are always grown-ups at home and at school who care about you and will help you make the right decision when you are confused. Remember, kids with character turn to grown-ups for help when they aren't sure what to do!

GOAL-OF-THE-WEEK DAILY MINI-LESSONS

WEEK 24
TOPIC: TRUTH/COURAGE
   GOAL: STAND UP FOR WHAT IS RIGHT

MONDAY: Remind students of our "Give me Five" goal – Always Do The Right Thing." Courage means doing the right thing, even when it's scary or difficult. It means following the rules – even when no one is looking and there is no chance of getting caught (like walking down an empty hallway, instead of running).

TUESDAY: Have you noticed someone being mean to someone else? How did you respond when that happened? Did you laugh? Did you join in? Did you pretend you didn't hear? If you did, you are part of the problem. Have the courage to SAY something ("Hey, leave her alone." "That's not kind!") or DO something (refuse to be a part of the meanness – walk away and invite the person who was the target to join you). Remind students of our school policy – we report anything that hurts, is dangerous, or makes you feel worried or afraid.

WEDNESDAY: Talk to students about the difference between being bossy and standing up for what is right. Someone who is bossy likes to have their own way – they want to make the rules, choose the game and tell others what they "should" be doing. When someone is standing up for what is right, they recognize that an injustice has occurred and they have the courage to do/say something about it.

THURSDAY: Standing up for what is right means being truthful about something that no one would ever know about (like returning money when you are given too much change.) Talk to students about the importance of "doing the right thing" – even though it might be scary or difficult to do.

FRIDAY: Sometimes we are confused about whether or not we should say or do something about a certain situation. In your attempts to make "right" choices, feel free to turn to a trusted adult for help to know what to do. Have children list names of trusted adults.

MORNING ANNOUNCEMENTS

GOAL: CONTROL YOUR ACTIONS

MONDAY: Hey kids! Did you know that it's OKAY to feel angry!!?? Just like happy, sad and excited, anger is just a feeling. It's what you DO when you feel angry that matters most. It's never okay to hurt someone's body, hurt their feelings or damage property when you feel angry. Kids with character learn how to feel mad in a way that is safe and doesn't hurt others.

TUESDAY: Hey kids! Mad isn't a feeling that most people like. Choosing to do something that helps calm mad feelings can make them go away really fast! The next time you are feeling mad, choose to do something that helps calm your mad feelings and you will feel better in no time!

WEDNESDAY: Hey kids! Did you know that if someone hurts you, or someone else, your job is to REPORT it to the grown up in charge? It's never okay to hurt someone's body, even if they hurt you first. Controlling your actions means that you never hurt another person, no matter what. When you Control Your Actions, you help everyone to be safe, AND you are showing your great character!

THURSDAY: Hey kids! Do you know what to do when you notice that someone is having trouble controlling their anger? It's probably best to walk away and find something else to do until they are calm. It's easiest to work out problems when people are calm and in control. Yelling back at someone is never helpful!! Your good character shows when you stay calm even when others are not!

FRIDAY: Hey kids! Would you like a tip for helping others – especially brothers and sisters - be nicer? Here it is…"DON'T DO IT BACK!" When someone does something to you that you don't like, DON'T DO IT BACK! If someone hurts you, DON'T DO IT BACK! If someone is mean to you, DON'T DO IT BACK! You are showing great character when you DON'T DO IT BACK.

WEEK 25
TOPIC: ANGER MANAGEMENT/SELF-CONTROL
GOAL: CONTROL YOUR ACTIONS

MONDAY: Feeling angry is okay! It's what you DO when you are angry that matters the most. It is never okay to hurt someone's feelings, body or property because you are angry. We learn how to behave when we are angry by watching others. Sometimes we forget that there might be a different (better) way to handle anger. Allow students to talk about how they've observed others handle their angry feelings—shouting, slamming, hitting, mean words, etc. Allow children to express how they feel when others are angry. This week we will be talking about a better way for you to handle your anger.

TUESDAY: Although it is okay to feel anger, it is not an emotion that we strive for or try to prolong. NO ONE LIKES TO FEEL MAD! When we feel angry, we can make a choice about how to respond. Choosing something "tight" like stomping, yelling, throwing ourselves (or things), punching a pillow, etc., are choices that often make our mad feelings grow. Demonstrate for children by stomping and yelling and have them notice the color of your face. Have them guess what your heart is doing (beating faster). When we feel angry and we choose something tight to do, our anger usually grows bigger.

On the other hand, choosing something "loose" to do (things that make us feel relaxed and happy) will help angry feelings go away and have you feeling better in no time! Brainstorm a list of "loose" things to do (sing a song, ride a bike, read a book, dance, play a game, etc.) to help angry feelings go away.

WEDNESDAY: If someone hurts your feelings or hurts your body, REPORT it to an adult. Hurting someone is never justified, even if they've hurt you first. Treat others the way you would like to be treated. If you know someone who has trouble being kind to others, try extra hard to show them how a kind friend behaves.

THURSDAY: If someone is expressing their angry feelings toward you in a "tight" way, you have two choices.

1) If it is a grown-up, the most respectful thing to do is say nothing. Acknowledge what they are saying to you with a head nod, (and perhaps a verbal "okay") and answer truthfully any questions you are being asked. Do not say, "But….," as it may just make the situation worse. Wait until the situation has calmed down to provide explanations.

2) If it is a sibling or peer, choose to walk away. Do not argue verbally or physically. Once the person is calm and in control, you may choose to return to work through the initial disagreement. Choosing something else to do is always a good idea and allows time for the situation to settle.

FRIDAY: When someone is angry, and behaving in a way that is hurtful to you or someone else, it's important to remember this important rule - **Don't Do it Back!** You are in control of you. No one can "make" you do something. Make a good choice. Help to make the situation better – **Don't Do it Back!** Talk about how children often justify their actions by saying, "He did it first!" It is never okay to hurt someone - even if they hurt you first.

MORNING ANNOUNCEMENTS

GOAL: CONTROL YOUR THOUGHTS

MONDAY: Hey kids! Did you know that the words you say inside your head can help to make you try your best and feel great about yourself? They can! Inside of your brain, try to tell yourself positive, encouraging words. When you look in the mirror, say to yourself, "I like myself. I'm glad I'm me." Having kind thoughts inside your head helps you to feel happy about your life and shows your great character!

TUESDAY: Hey kids! Remember the story of "The Little Engine That Could?" When he was trying to pull the train up the mountain, he said the words "I think I can, I think I can." When something is hard for you, saying "I think I can, I think I can" helps make what you are trying to do easier. Try it next time and see what a difference it makes!

WEDNESDAY: Hey kids! Are you someone who worries a lot? Did you know that the words that you say inside your head can help take your worries away? The next time you are feeling worried about something, try saying to yourself, "Everything is going to be fine….I know what to do if I need help." Kids with character say positive words like these to help keep worries small.

THURSDAY: Hey kids! Can you remember the last time you felt mad? Did you know that it's okay to be mad, but it's NOT okay to be mean? When you are feeling mad, saying calm words inside your head helps make your anger smaller. Kids with great character know that it's okay to feel mad, but they also work hard to make their mad shrink instead of grow.

FRIDAY: Hey kids! Do you know what it means when someone says, "Look on the bright side?" It means that you think positive thoughts. When your trip to the movies gets postponed for another day, someone who thinks positively might say, "It's okay that we can't go today. "At least we can still go another day." Your good character really shows when you think positive thoughts!

WEEK 26
TOPIC: ANGER MANAGEMENT/SELF-CONTROL
GOAL: CONTROL YOUR THOUGHTS

MONDAY: Talk about (and explain to young students) about the internal dialogue that we have with ourselves. (Words that we say inside our heads about how we feel about ourselves and others.) Discuss the importance of having a positive internal dialogue with ourselves, and the impact that it has on our feelings (vs. a negative internal dialogue and the resulting feelings.) Encourage children to talk positively to themselves about the personal characteristics that make them different from others. ("I love my freckles. My mom's friend Barb is beautiful and she has freckles all over her whole body! I must be beautiful too!" instead of, "I don't like my freckles and I wish I never had them.")

TUESDAY: There's a lot to be said about an "I think I can" spirit. There once was a boy who struggled when it came to spelling (tying his shoe – depending on the age of the group). Even though he studied for his tests (practiced and practiced tying), he never seemed to do very well on them. One day the teacher asked to speak to the boy before the test. She asked him about the words he said to himself while he was taking his tests. The boy explained that he usually said something like, "I hate spelling. I'm terrible at it. I will probably get all the words wrong." ("I can't tie. It's too hard. I will probably never learn how to tie.") By the time the boy got done with the test, he was feeling pretty discouraged. The teacher asked the boy if he would try something different this time. She said, "During your spelling test today, I want you to say to yourself, 'I can do it! I will try my best and take my time! I KNOW I can do it!" The spelling test was still hard for the boy, but he wasn't as frustrated as he usually was when it was over. The teacher noticed that his handwriting seemed much neater than usual and he had done better than ever before! From then on, every time the boy took a test, he gave himself positive words of encouragement so that he could do his best.

WEDNESDAY: Sometimes the worries that children have come from the words that they say to themselves about what might happen. For example, the phone might ring in your classroom and the teacher says that you are wanted in the principal's office. As you walk to the principal's office, the words inside your head are saying, "Oh no! I must be in big trouble! My mom and dad are going to be so mad at me! I bet I will be grounded." By the time you reach the office, you are feeling so sick to your stomach that you almost couldn't hear him sing happy birthday to you! PRACTICE POSITVE THOUGHTS!

THURSDAY: When others are expressing anger towards us, it is common to have negative thoughts like, "She's so mean! She always yells at me and tells me to go to my room and no one else ever gets in trouble. It's just not fair!" Does having negative thoughts in your head make your anger grow bigger or help it get smaller? (Bigger.) What other words could you say inside your head to help keep you calm and that would help you to understand how the other person is feeling? ("She's angry because she wants me to: do my best, follow the rules, be safe, have friends, etc. I know that she loves me and wants the best for me.")

FRIDAY: Talk to kids about having an optimistic outlook on life. Discuss "Looking on the bright side" or share the example of a glass filled to the half way mark with milk. Is it half empty or half full? Teaching children how to dialogue positively to themselves will help them to manage their anger, worries, and give them the courage to keep on trying to be their personal best.

MORNING ANNOUNCEMENTS

WEEK 27

GOAL: STOP AND THINK

MONDAY: Hey kids! Would you like a tip to help you when you are feeling angry? A tip that will help you to make a good choice and stay out of trouble when you are feeling mad? The next time you start to feel angry…remember to…. STOP. When you STOP it gives your brain a minute to catch up and make a good choice for what to do next. Kids with character know that it's okay to FEEL mad, and they remember to STOP and THINK when they feel mad.

TUESDAY: Hey kids! Our goal this week is Stop and Think! When you start to feel angry, Stop and Think about your breathing. Take a slow, deep breath in, and slowly blow all of the air out. Taking some deep breaths when you feel angry helps you feel better and allows your great character to shine through!

WEDNESDAY: Hey kids! The next time you start feeling mad, STOP and try counting slowly to ten. Counting slowly sounds like this: 1…..2…..3……4……and so on. Once you get really good at it, you can probably count inside of your head so that no one can hear you. Kids with character practice ways to feel better when they have mad feelings.

THURSDAY: Hey kids! Let's review what to do the next time you start to feel mad…Step one is STOP. When you remember to STOP, you give your brain a minute to catch up so that you can make a choice that will help. Taking a deep breath or counting slowly to ten are two "loose" choices that help make your anger get smaller. Show your good character the next time you start to feel mad by remembering to STOP and choose something "loose" to do.

FRIDAY: Hey kids! Remember that FEELING mad is just part of life. Knowing what to do when you start to feel mad can make the difference between feeling better quickly – or feeling worse and possibly even getting yourself in trouble. The next time you begin to feel mad, make sure you STOP and CHOOSE SOMETHING LOOSE to do. And don't forget that very important tip to help make the world be a better place! When someone does something that you don't like, **DON'T DO IT BACK!**

WEEK 27
TOPIC: ANGER MANAGEMENT/SELF-CONTROL
GOAL: STOP & THINK

MONDAY: When we feel angry, it's usually the behaviors we choose (in response to the feeling) that gets us into trouble. We forget to take a moment to think about a good way to respond! Teach children that the FIRST thing to do when they feel themselves starting to become mad is STOP! Do not throw things. Do not stomp. Do not yell. Do not slam doors! Just STOP for a moment and think about your best next step. Students would benefit from having the adult model this; demonstrate between an immediate, impulsive response, and a "STOP" followed by a composed response.

TUESDAY: Once you STOP do an internal check on your breathing. Since holding your breath is a "tight" thing to do (and will help you to hold on to the anger) it's important that you check to be sure that you are breathing. While you're at it, take a few slow, deep breaths in and out. Practice deep breathing with the kids.

WEDNESDAY: Count to 10 (or 20 or 100) as you consider your best next step. Slowly breathe in and breathe out and make certain that you are doing your best to talk positively with yourself during this time. If someone is yelling at you… STOP and look at them. Say nothing…or be truthful if someone is asking a question…but keep it simple.

THURSDAY: When you choose to "STOP" you give your brain a minute to catch up. Taking a deep breath and counting gives you a moment to think about what a good choice might be. Review respectful responses to common classroom altercations like budging in line, unkind facial expressions/remarks, etc. Remind children about keeping hands and feet to themselves for safety (and to keep themselves out of trouble) – and our **commitment** to making the world a kinder place by choosing, **DON'T DO IT BACK!**

FRIDAY: STAR stands for Stop, Think and Respond. When you are feeling angry, STOP and THINK. Respond by choosing something loose to do and use positive words inside of your head so that you will be feeling better in no time!

MORNING ANNOUNCEMENTS

GOAL: BE IN CHARGE OF YOURSELF

MONDAY: Hey kids! Did you know that we have rules and laws to help keep people safe and happy? Part of BEING IN CHARGE OF YOURSELF means that you LEARN about rules and laws and make sure that you are following them at all times. Show your great character by BEING IN CHARGE OF YOURSELF and following rules and laws.

TUESDAY: Hey kids! BEING IN CHARGE OF YOURSELF means that you are in charge of YOU and no one else!! It is your job to make sure YOU are doing what YOU are supposed to be doing. It is NOT your job to make sure that everyone else is doing their jobs! (That's called bossy!) Show your great character by making sure YOU are doing what you are supposed to do… and let the grown-ups take care of giving reminders to others if they are needed.

WEDNESDAY: Hey kids! It's important to be in charge of yourself by controlling your body at all times! That means that you keep your hands and feet to yourself, and you do your best to ignore it when others are moving or making sounds that distract you. Kids with great character control their bodies at all times!

THURSDAY: Hey kids! Practice showing respect by being a good listener. Do you remember the steps? Step one is to look at the person talking, step two is to stay still and step three is to think about what the person is saying. Your great character shines through every time you choose to be a respectful listener.

FRIDAY: Hey kids! This week we've been talking about all of the different things that you are in charge of to help you have a great day. REMEMBERING all of the things you need to do can sometimes be hard. Have you ever tried to write yourself a note to help you remember the important things you need to do? Grown ups do it all the time! When kids work hard to remember things like homework, school notes and library books, it shows RESPONSIBILITY, which is a terrific way to demonstrate your great character.

WEEK 28
TOPIC: ANGER MANAGEMENT/SELF-CONTROL
GOAL: BE IN CHARGE OF YOURSELF

MONDAY: Be in charge of YOU! Pay attention to rules at home and at school and work hard to follow them. (Give kids a chance to name some of the rules in both places.) Talk about the consequences when rules are broken.

TUESDAY: Remind students that their job is to manage themselves, and not manage others. Unless they observe something that poses a serious danger to themselves or someone else, they should refrain from going to adults about the failure of others to follow rules. Give examples of times when this is commonly forgotten at school. ("Teacher, he's not cleaning up!" "She ran down the hall!)

WEDNESDAY: It is a distraction to others when someone is constantly moving about. When someone is talking, look at the speaker and hold your hands and feet still. Do your best to ignore the sounds and movements of others. Keep your hands and feet to yourself when you are waiting/walking in line. It is your job to be in control of your body at all times!

THURSDAY: When instructions are being given, look at the person speaking and LISTEN carefully so that you will know what to do.
Remind students the steps to being a respectful listener:

      1.) Look at the person talking
      2.) Stay still
      3.) Think (about what the person is saying)

Repeat the instructions in your head. Write down some notes if you think that you won't be able to remember. Respond to the instructions immediately. Don't allow yourself to get sidetracked. Don't rely on others to know what you are supposed to be doing. YOU take care of YOU!

FRIDAY: If there is something you need to remember to do or bring to school, write it down in your agenda. Get in the habit of checking your book bag daily for homework assignments and notes of reminders. Do not rely on your friends to remind you about special events or assignments. Bring your own materials and supplies to school. Although everyone might forget something every once in awhile (and we all are willing to share) others become frustrated when they are relied on too frequently because classmates just "forget."

MORNING ANNOUNCEMENTS

WEEK 29

GOAL: MAKE GOOD CHOICES!

MONDAY: Hey kids! There are so many important choices that you get to make every single day. Did you know that something as small as a smile, a greeting, or offering to help someone in a small way can make a BIG difference in someone's day? Being cheerful and kind is a great way to show others your great attitude! Try extra hard to make friendly choices today and see what a difference it makes!

TUESDAY: Hey kids! A wonderful choice that you get to make every day is CHOOSING KINDNESS. Did you realize that KINDNESS is a choice? In addition to being friendly and helping others whenever you can, you can choose kind, gentle words when talking to others. Using a kind, gentle voice shows caring and respect to others and lets your great character shine through!

WEDNESDAY: Hey kids! Another great choice to make is to TELL THE TRUTH. Mistakes are just part of life and when you choose to tell the TRUTH you are showing others that good character is important to you.

THURSDAY: Hey kids! Isn't it wonderful when others forgive our mistakes? Show your great character today by choosing to forgive someone ELSE when THEY make a mistake. Choosing to forgive is another easy way to let others know that we understand that everyone makes mistakes.

FRIDAY: Hey kids! Did you know that another great choice to make is to choose to be responsible? Being responsible means that you take care of your belongings at home and at school; take care of keeping your hair, teeth and body clean and go to bed without making a fuss. Other ways to show that you are responsible are to: be on time; keep your word; always do the right thing and be the kind of friend you would like to have. Your great character shines through when you make good choices in your life.

GOAL-OF-THE-WEEK DAILY MINI-LESSONS

WEEK 29
TOPIC: MAKING CHOICES
 GOAL: MAKE GOOD CHOICES!

MONDAY: No matter what grade level your students are, there are so many important **choices** to make every day! Talk to children about choosing to smile, greet others, offer to help, be kind to others. Being cheerful and kind is a great way to show others your great attitude! Not doing so well in the attitude department? It's never too late to decide you would like to behave differently. Challenge students to exaggerate these things and to notice the positive responses they receive.

TUESDAY: Choose to be **kind!** Did you even realize that kindness is a choice that you get to make every single day? Discuss the difference between grouchy words/grouchy tone ("STOP IT!"); kind words with a grouchy tone (scream, "Would you PLEASE stop it?"); and kind words with a kind tone (gently say, "Could you please stop singing? It's bothering me.") Can anyone MAKE you speak with grouchy words/tone......or is it a choice?

WEDNESDAY: Choose to be **truthful**. If you make a mistake at home, tell the truth! If you make a mistake on the bus, tell the truth! If you make a mistake at school, tell the truth! If you make a mistake with your friends, tell the truth! NO ONE is expected to be perfect. Show your good character by showing others that being honest is important to you.

THURSDAY: Choose to offer **forgiveness**. We all know what it's like to make mistakes and want the forgiveness of others. Please offer your own forgiveness when someone apologizes to you. Remind students that it is important to work hard not to make the same mistakes over and over. Since everyone makes mistakes, it's important that we get really, really good at apologizing and offering forgiveness. (No grudge holding allowed!)

FRIDAY: Make the choice to be **responsible**. Choose to take good care of your personal items at home and at school. Keep your body/hair clean. Choose to keep a tidy room and to do your chores without being reminded. Go to bed on time, without a fuss.

Choose to do your best work in school. When you are writing, write in your neatest handwriting. When you finish your math, check your answers over carefully. Check to be sure that your name is at the top and that you haven't left any answers blank. If you don't understand, ask for help from an adult.

Additional responsibilities to mention/include in discussion: following rules, coming to school on time, keeping your word, being a good friend to others, etc.

MORNING ANNOUNCEMENTS

GOAL: AGREE TO BE...SCREEN FREE!

MONDAY: Hey kids! SCREEN FREE WEEK will be starting soon. HIP, HIP HOORAY!! That will give us a chance to enjoy all the wonderful things in our lives that do NOT involve a screen. You show great character when you TRY something new. Do YOU have the courage to TRY? I sure hope so!!

TUESDAY: Hey kids! SCREEN FREE WEEK is coming soon! It lasts for seven days. How many days do you think YOU can be screen free? Some students say that they are going to set a record for being screen free. Are you one of them?? Remember, that no matter how you do, the MOST important thing is that you TELL THE TRUTH. Being truthful shows your great character!

WEDNESDAY: Hey kids! SCREEN FREE WEEK is coming soon! Do you know WHY we even have SCREEN FREE WEEK? It's not because all of those SCREEN activities are bad...it's because TOO MANY of those screen activities are bad!! Fun and healthy activities are a much better way to spend our time. Think about all of the great things you can do when you turn off those screens!

THURSDAY: Hey kids! Are you getting excited about SCREEN FREE WEEK? I sure am! We're going to have fun being more active. It's going to be GREAT fun!! I hope you'll try your best along with the rest of us!

FRIDAY: Hey kids! SCREEN FREE WEEK will start when you wake up for school on MONDAY! We will all do our best to be SCREEN FREE for SEVEN whole days! Have you started to think about all the fun things you want to do during SCREEN FREE WEEK? You might want to start making a list!

GOAL-OF-THE-WEEK DAILY MINI-LESSONS

WEEK 30
TOPIC: MAKING CHOICES
GOAL: AGREE TO BE...SCREEN FREE!

MONDAY: SCREEN FREE WEEK is coming! It will begin next week! Review rules for the week…No television, video games, dvds, movies, computer anythings (games, e-mail, facebook), gameboy, cell phones, – unless it is required for school (starting next MONDAY!). Encourage those who resist to "give it a try." Even if they only make it through a day or two, they should feel proud that they were willing to try. Ask children to make a promise to "do their best" and no matter what – tell the truth about their involvement (or lack of).

TUESDAY: Have students set a goal for themselves for SCREEN FREE WEEK. Share your own personal goal. Share honestly about what will be hardest for you. Ask children to make a promise to "do their best" and no matter what – tell the truth about their involvement (or lack of).

WEDNESDAY: Why do we have SCREEN FREE WEEK? Certainly, all screen use is not bad but spending too much time in front of the various "screens" in our lives prevents us from participating in other fun, healthy activities. Allow children time to share the fun things they are going to do while they are enjoying being screen free.

THURSDAY: Spend some time talking about ratings of movies and video games. As they grow many children perceive "G" rated movies and "E" rated video games to be solely for "little kids." Share your personal enjoyment of material with this rating—and you are a grown-up!. Discourage exposure to scary/horror/violent type media.

FRIDAY: Allow students to share the difficulties/challenges they anticipate in their efforts to be screen free. Allow classmates to support one another by offering suggestions to those who might have difficulties. Have students share their plans for being screen free.

MORNING ANNOUNCEMENTS

WEEK 31

GOAL: TURN OFF THOSE SCREENS, TURN ON LIFE!

MONDAY: Hey kids! SCREEN FREE WEEK is here! It started this morning when you woke up and will continue for SEVEN days! Only SEVEN - not SEVEN HUNDRED! We are going to do our very best to find lots of fun and creative SCREEN FREE things to do this week. Remember—there are only two important rules: try your best and tell the truth. Have a great week!

TUESDAY: Hey kids! How was your first day of SCREEN FREE WEEK? I hope you did something fun that you haven't done in a l-o-n-g time. One day down, six to go. You can do it!!

WEDNESDAY: Hey kids! This is our third day of SCREEN FREE WEEK already! After today, we're almost half way done! There are so many fun things to do when you are a kid! Keep working to find some new and interesting things to do this week.

THURSDAY: Hey kids! After today, there are only three days left of SCREEN FREE WEEK! Are you remembering the two important rules? Your great character shines through when you remember to try your best and tell the truth during SCREEN FREE WEEK.

FRIDAY: Hey kids! I know lots of you have worked very hard this week to keep those screens off. Hooray for you! Remember to keep those screens off until you wake up Monday morning! YOU CAN DO IT! Congratulations on a great week!

GOAL-OF-THE-WEEK
DAILY MINI-LESSONS

WEEK 31
TOPIC: MAKING CHOICES
GOAL: TURN OFF THOSE SCREENS, TURN ON LIFE!

MONDAY: Today is the first day of SCREEN FREE WEEK! Have students set a goal for themselves and make a plan for success. Having a plan in writing (or for the little ones, even signing their name to a pledge sheet) helps them to avoid the temptations of the week.

Review rules for SCREEN FREE WEEK…No TV, video games, dvds, movies, computer anythings, gameboy or cell phones—unless it is required for school. Encourage those who resist to "give it a try." Even if they only make it through a day or two, they should feel proud that they were willing to try. Ask children to make a promise to "do their best" and no matter what— tell the truth about their involvement (or lack of).

TUESDAY: How did you do yesterday? What was the hardest thing about keeping those screens off? What is something that you did that you might not have otherwise done?   Why do we have SCREEN FREE WEEK? Certainly, all Screen acitivities are not bad but spending too much time in front of the various screens in our lives prevents us from participating in other fun, healthy activities. Allow children time to share the fun things they are doing while they are enjoying being screen free.

WEDNESDAY: Explain what "Turn Off Those Screens, Turn on Life" means. (That while you are busy watching TV, playing video games, etc.,, your life is passing you by. You are not using your time to learn, get exercise, be healthy, or help others. You are WASTING your time!)   When you are young, you don't have to deal with adult worries. You don't worry about making dinner, paying bills or the flat tire on the car. You get to run and play and have fun. Don't waste these years in front of a screen!

THURSDAY: Ask children how they are doing? Is it hard or easy to be screen free? Talk about the feeling of pride we have when we try to do something hard and we are successful. It feels GREAT! Allow children to share the "non-screen" related activities that they are participating in. Allow children to share the fun that they are having as they, "Turn off Those Screens and Turn on Life!"

FRIDAY: Continue THURSDAY's conversations. Allow students to share the difficulties/challenges they anticipate in their efforts to be screen free through the weekend. Allow classmates to support one another by offering suggestions to those who might have difficulties.   Allow students to share "non-screen" related weekend plans. Share your own.

MORNING ANNOUNCEMENTS

GOAL: SMILE AND SHOW YOUR GREAT ATTITUDE!

MONDAY: Hey kids! I noticed lots of smiles walking in our building with you this morning. Were you wearing one? Did you know that when I see someone smile, I think they are friendly, happy, and kind? Remember to wear your smile to show others your good character!

TUESDAY: Hey kids! Did you know that smiles are contagious? Do you know what that means? It means that when YOU smile, other people feel like smiling too!! Give it a try today! Smile at everyone you see and notice how many people smile back at you!!

WEDNESDAY: Hey kids! Is there someone that you are wishing to be friends with? Let me give you an easy tip for starting that friendship....SMILE!! Everyone likes to know happy, friendly people, and you never know...your smile could be the beginning of a beautiful friendship!

THURSDAY: Hey kids! Did you know that smiling can make you feel better? If you are having a rough day – even if you don't feel like it, try smiling your brightest smile. Having a smile on your face will help you to feel better in no time!

FRIDAY: Hey kids! Do you know what a smiley voice sounds like? It's a voice that sounds cheerful and happy. Do you know someone who has a smiley voice? Having a smile in your voice is a great way to show respect and spread joy to the people around you.

WEEK 32
TOPIC: POSITIVE ATTITUDE
  GOAL: SMILE AND SHOW YOUR GREAT ATTITUDE

MONDAY: Talk with students about how the expression you wear on your face sends a message to those around you, without ever having to utter a word. It is the initial piece of information we receive about others that helps us decide if we would like to get to know someone better. Solicit from students the "impression" they get from someone who is smiling all of the time (nice, friendly, helpful, happy, etc.). Compare that to the "impression" they get about someone who is not smiling. Challenge students to think about the "impression" they give others.

TUESDAY: As the class waits for you to begin, smile at your students and say nothing. Just look at them and smile. Make mental notes of what occurs…Smiles are contagious! When you smile a bright, cheerful smile at someone, *even without ever speaking a word*, almost always that person will smile back at you. Do an experiment and report back your findings.

WEDNESDAY: Smiling helps us to make connections with the people around us. It keeps us from remaining separate from one another. Even babies as young as three weeks old recognize smiling as a bonding behavior. Would you like to be friends with someone new? Smiling at them often is a great way to start.

THURSDAY: Smiling makes you feel better! Are you having a rough day? The next time you are feeling less than cheerful, try this experiment: smile your brightest smile. You will be amazed at how quickly you begin to feel better! It's almost like magic! (Note to Leader) Research has shown that a genuine smile increases the production of serotonin, the happy hormone.

FRIDAY: Allow your smile to spill over into your voice. What does a smiley voice sound like? Give students examples of how to answer the phone with a smile in your voice. What "impression" do you get from someone who *sounds* smiley? Ask students how to respond to parent and/or teacher requests with a smile in their voice. Why would this be advantageous?

Interesting tidbit: What a workout! One smile uses more than 16 muscles!

MORNING ANNOUNCEMENTS

GOAL: WORK HARD

MONDAY: Hey kids! Did you ever want to learn how to do something new or get better at something you already know how to do? Setting a goal and working hard towards the things that are important to you are necessary steps to making your dreams come true. Working hard TODAY is a wonderful way to show your great character AND help reach your goals!

TUESDAY: Hey kids! One way to show that you are a hard worker is to check your work. Don't rush. Read over your school work before you hand it in and fix any mistakes that you find. Checking your work doesn't take much time and it shows that you are proud of your work and want to do your best!

WEDNESDAY: Hey kids! Part of working hard means that when you have a job, you take your time so that you can be sure that you do the job right. Working carefully on your school work and on your other jobs at home and at school shows your great character and helps to be sure that mistakes aren't made.

THURSDAY: Hey kids! Did you ever try to do something that was hard for you? Tying your shoe, riding a two-wheeler and swimming are things that lots of kids are trying to learn. When you try and try and keep on trying while you are learning something new, your positive attitude shines through and you will be able to learn your new skill faster.

FRIDAY: Hey kids! Remember that while you are working hard, it's important to always put your best foot forward. Do you know what that means? That means that no matter what you are doing, you try your very best. Kids with outstanding character work hard and try their best in everything they do!

GOAL-OF-THE-WEEK DAILY MINI-LESSONS

WEEK 33
TOPIC: POSITIVE ATTITUDE
GOAL: WORK HARD

MONDAY: Ask students about their goals and dreams they have for their lives. Share a goal that you had for yourself when you were little, and have realized as an adult. Tell them that working hard *today* is the first step in reaching their goals and making their dreams come true. Make a connection between working hard and achieving one of your own goals.

TUESDAY: Be proud of the way your work looks! Talk to students about the neatness of their work and the importance of checking it over for grammar and/or spelling errors. The way you write and present yourself on paper is sometimes the first way that someone gets to know you. Every single time you hand in something to your teacher it should represent your best effort.

WEDNESDAY: Have a discussion about not rushing and checking over work before handing it in. Ask how many of them have ever made "careless" mistakes. Explain what that means (you either knew the answer, or knew how to find the answer, but made a silly mistake that resulted in the wrong answer.) Taking your time and checking over your work ensures that careless mistakes aren't made.

THURSDAY: Have an "I think I can" spirit. Part of being and doing your best and reaching your goals is never giving up. Didn't do so well on something? Don't be discouraged! The most successful people are those who pick themselves up and try again – even after they have been unsuccessful. Figure out what you have to do differently next time to be successful. And then….DO IT!

FRIDAY: Talk to students about "being the best they can be"; not settling for less than their best; taking their time; giving their all; hanging in there. If you are willing to work hard and do your best, great things are sure to happen!

MORNING ANNOUNCEMENTS

WEEK 34

GOAL: DON'T GIVE UP

MONDAY: Hey kids! Remember the story of, *The Little Engine that Could*? When she had a job that was hard to do, she said these words to herself…"I think I can, I think I can…" Show your terrific character by saying those same words, "I think I can, I think I can" the next time you try something new. It really does help to make things easier!

TUESDAY: Hey kids! Everyone needs a little help from time to time. When have you needed help before? Did you know who to go to for help? Knowing who to ask for help when you need it is important. The grown-up in charge is a great person to ask if you ever need help with something.

WEDNESDAY: Hey kids! Did you know that thinking positive thoughts when something is hard will help you get the job done? The next time you are practicing something that you just learned, try saying this, "I will do my best" or "I'll keep on trying." When something is hard, saying positive words to yourself helps your heart and your brain to keep on trying. The best part is that you will find out that most things are not so hard after all!

THURSDAY: Hey kids! Have you ever heard of the word perseverance? Perseverance is a word that means to never give up, keep on trying and to hang in there. Kids with character don't give up when something is hard. They keep on trying…and trying…and trying. How about you? Do you persevere when something is hard?

FRIDAY: Hey kids! Do you know what determined means? Kids who are determined don't stop trying until they succeed. When you do your very best, keep on trying, never give up, and believe in yourself, you show determination AND you achieve your goals!

GOAL-OF-THE-WEEK DAILY MINI-LESSONS

WEEK 34
TOPIC: POSITIVE ATTITUDE
GOAL: DON'T GIVE UP

MONDAY: Start your day with, "I CAN!" Recall the story of *The Little Engine that Could*. Talk about having an "I can do it" spirit. Give examples of school related instances where it is beneficial to have a "never give up" attitude.

TUESDAY: Discuss who to go to if ever in need of help. Identify appropriate adults in and out of school that are there to help with both academic and social/emotional difficulties. Don't forget to mention and encourage children to discuss any difficulties they are having with their parents.

WEDNESDAY: When we feel discouraged, we often engage in destructive thinking. When you say to yourself, "I'm not very good at this," "This is too hard," or "I'll never understand or be able to do this" – you surely will not. Talk to students about the negative "self-talk" that they engage in. Provide them with some examples of positive self-talk ("I can do this." "I know I can." "I'll keep on trying.") and encourage them to try it the next time they are struggling. They might be surprised by how much it helps!

THURSDAY: Introduce the word *perseverance* (determination). Discuss some of the quotes below:

- "I do the best I know how – the very best I can; and I mean to keep on doing so until the end." – *Abraham Lincoln*

- "The difference between the possible and the impossible lies in a person's determination." – *Tommy Lasorda*

- "The harder you work the luckier you get." – *Gary Player*

- "Perseverance is not a long race; it is many short races one after another." – *Walter Elliott*

FRIDAY: Ask students to think how it feels when they really want something badly for themselves or another person (like winning a sports event, buying something at the store, saving up allowance to buy a present for mom or dad, etc.). What would they do to achieve that goal? Discuss how perseverance and determination pay off for those who struggle to meet their goals.

MORNING ANNOUNCEMENTS

GOAL: BE A GOOD SPORT

MONDAY: Hey kids! Do you know what a "good sport" is? A good sport is someone who plays by the rules and has a good attitude whether they win or lose. Good sports support their favorite teams, but never root against – or "boo" other teams. Show your great character the next time you play a game by being a good sport.

TUESDAY: Hey kids! Being a good sport means that you are a polite winner. Do you know what that means? It means when you succeed at something, you don't brag or make fun of the mistakes that others make. Polite winners compliment others for trying their best and doing a good job. Show your great character by being a good sport and using good manners when you win!

WEDNESDAY: Hey kids! Yesterday we talked about the importance of being a polite winner. Did you know that it's also important to be a polite loser? Do you know what that means? Polite losers never pout, stomp, throw things or blame others. They compliment others by saying, "good game" and feel happy that they got to play. Show your great character by being polite the next time you lose at something.

THURSDAY: Hey kids! An important part of sportsmanship is teamwork. Working together as a team means that all of the team members are trying to make the same thing happen. Sharing and taking turns are very important when it comes to teamwork. Your great character shines through when you work peacefully with the other members on your team.

FRIDAY: Hey kids! Being a good sport means that when you are playing on a team, you are kind and supportive. Good sports never yell at, blame or laugh at their team members—instead, they help and encourage their team. Being a good sport shows wonderful character and helps everyone to have more fun!

GOAL-OF-THE-WEEK DAILY MINI-LESSONS

WEEK 35
TOPIC: POSITIVE ATTITUDE
GOAL: BE A GOOD SPORT

MONDAY: Explain to students what being a good sport means: Doing your best, playing fair (by the rules), being a good winner and a good loser, having a positive attitude, rooting in support of (never against). Allow students to provide examples of sportsmanship that they have experienced.

TUESDAY: Have a conversation with students about what a "good winner" looks and sounds like. A "good winner" never brags about their victory or makes fun of the failures of opponents. A good winner acknowledges and/or compliments others for their efforts and accomplishments. Being a good sport means that you sometimes play down your enthusiasm for winning (at least temporarily) so that you don't make someone else feel bad.

WEDNESDAY: Talk with students about what being a "good loser" looks and sounds like. A "good loser" does not pout or place blame on others for the outcome. They do not stomp feet, throw things or make excuses. They compliment others for their efforts and are happy just to have had the opportunity to play. Remind students, "If you had fun…you WON!"

THURSDAY: Part of sportsmanship is teamwork. Talk with students about teamwork— coming together to accomplish a common goal. Poor sportsmanship during team play is selfish. It might look like an unwillingness to pass the ball or give others a turn (or their "fair share" of having a turn). It sends a message that "I" am more important than "We." It draws attention away from the team effort and towards individuals. Include a discussion of quotes below, as appropriate for your grade level.

- "Alone we can do so little; together we can do so much." – *Helen Keller*

- "The law of life should not be competition, but cooperation, the good of each contributing to the good of all." - *Jawahardal Nehrue*

- "Individuals play the game, but teams win championships." - *Anonymous*

FRIDAY: Have a discussion with students about sportsmanship as it relates to how we treat our teammates. A good sport is encouraging to teammates. Someone who is showing good sportsmanship never yells at, blames or makes fun of teammates for making mistakes. A good sport offers words of encouragement to others and works hard to be sure that all players feel good about their involvement.

MORNING ANNOUNCEMENTS

GOAL: WEAR A HELMET

MONDAY: Hey kids! Do you know why it's so important to wear a helmet on your head whenever you ride your bike, roller blade, skateboard, ride a scooter, ski or ice skate? The reason is because inside of your head is your brain, and that's a very, VERY important part of your body. Kids with character make a safe choice when they enjoy certain activities by wearing a helmet.

TUESDAY: Hey kids! Do you know the test to see if your helmet is fastened tight enough? It's the "open mouth" test! After your helmet is on your head, and your strap is securely fastened under your chin, open your mouth as wide as you can. If you can feel your helmet squish down on your head when you open your mouth, you are good to go! Kids with character make sure they are safe before they enjoy outdoor activities.

WEDNESDAY: Hey kids! Do you know what an accident is? An accident is when something unexpected happens. We feel shocked and surprised when an accident happens because we didn't think it would! Show your great character by protecting your head in case an accident happens.

THURSDAY: Hey kids! Once you have your head protected with a helmet that fits you properly, it's important that you choose to ride somewhere safe. Choose a spot where there are no cars around or rocks/branches on the ground. Having a grown-up with you when you ride is another great way to make sure you will be safe while you play.

FRIDAY: Hey kids! Did you know that riding a bike that is too big for you can be dangerous? If it's too big it can be hard to control and increase the risk of a crash. Also, make sure that you tell an adult if your brakes aren't working right, if the seat is loose, or if you hear a rattling noise. Kids with character know how to keep themselves safe while riding.

GOAL-OF-THE-WEEK
DAILY MINI-LESSONS

WEEK 36
TOPIC: BE SAFE FOR THE SUMMER
  GOAL: WEAR A HELMET

MONDAY: Conversations this week surround the need for every single child to wear a helmet when participating in an activity where severe head injury is possible. Talk about why it is so important to protect your brain – because your brain is in charge of making you walk, talk and move the way you do. Brainstorm the variety of activities that this would include—riding bikes, scooters, rollerblades, skates, skateboards, dirt bikes – even skiing and horseback riding.

TUESDAY: The helmet should cover the child's forehead and fit snugly in a level position. Teach them the "open mouth test." After your helmet is fastened safely under your chin, open your mouth as wide as you can. If opening your mouth causes the helmet to squish down on your head, it's tight enough. If not, it's not tight enough. Have an adult help with proper fitting so that your head is protected.

WEDNESDAY: Have a discussion with students about accidents. What does it mean to have an accident? Obviously, it is something unexpected/unplanned/ unwanted that happens. No one knows when an accident will happen. Otherwise, we might call them "on purposes" instead of accidents. Many, many, many people (even adults!) have had accidents when they were riding without a helmet. Share/solicit stories of unexpected things that have happened while riding. The only way to be certain your precious brain is protected is to wear a properly fitted helmet each time you ride.

THURSDAY: Ride in safe places! The best place to ride is a wide, flat surface – where there are no cars or debris. Sidewalk riding is safe only when a grown-up is next to you to help recognize and stop for hazards – cars backing out of driveways, pedestrians, shrubs or fences that obscure vision, debris, and uneven or broken surfaces.

FRIDAY: Although it might be fun to ride a big brother/sister's bike, bikes that don't fit are hard to control and increase the risk of a crash. Make sure you ask an adult for help if you notice that the brakes aren't working right, the seat is loose or you hear a rattling noise.

MORNING ANNOUNCEMENTS

GOAL: WEAR YOUR SEAT BELT

MONDAY: Hey kids! Do you know the safest place for you to ride when you are riding in the car? That's right!! It's the BACK seat of the car. If you have a van, the middle seat is also safe. Kids with character keep themselves safe by sitting in the back seat every single time they ride in the car.

TUESDAY: Hey kids! Once you are safely sitting in the backseat of the car, don't forget that seatbelt! Sitting in a car seat or booster seat that is strapped in is a great way to stay safe while you ride. If you are too big for a booster seat, make sure you fasten your seatbelt and face the front of the car while you are riding. Your great character shows when you make safe riding choices for yourself!

WEDNESDAY: Hey kids! When you are riding in a car, it's very important that you sit still and stay quiet. Arguing and fooling around can make it harder for the driver to pay attention to the road and cause an accident. Your good character shines when you are a respectful passenger when you ride.

THURSDAY: Hey kids! Keep yourself safe while you're riding by staying buckled and in your seat at all times! Getting up while the car is still moving can be extremely dangerous! Kids with character keep themselves safe by staying seated at all times while the car is moving.

FRIDAY: Hey kids! Make sure you keep all of your body parts INSIDE the car at all times. Hanging any body parts out of a window can be a VERY dangerous thing to do. Your good character shows every time you are safe and respectful when you ride.

GOAL-OF-THE-WEEK DAILY MINI-LESSONS

WEEK 37
TOPIC: BE SAFE FOR THE SUMMER
GOAL: WEAR YOUR SEAT BELT

MONDAY: Reinforce with students that the safest place for them to ride is the back seat of the vehicle. When riding in a van, the middle or back seat is fine. When riding in a truck that does not have a back seat, it is safest to sit in the front seat with a seatbelt (as opposed to sitting in the truck bed). Tell children to share this important safety rule with the grown ups that they ride with.

TUESDAY: Talk to children about remaining facing forward with a seatbelt on snuggly while they are riding in a motor vehicle. Remind them that we never know when an accident might happen, so it's important to be safe at all times.

WEDNESDAY: Have a discussion with children about being a respectful passenger. No arguing or goofing around; talk quietly so that the driver can concentrate on safe driving; remain seated; never throw anything.

THURSDAY: While the car is moving, don't unbuckle for any reason! Talk about the momentum of passengers any time the driver slams on the brakes, and the many different reasons why that might happen. Allow children to share stories of what happened when they have been unbuckled. Stay seated until the car is turned off.

FRIDAY: Keep all body parts inside the vehicle at all times. Have children share/ brainstorm quiet, safe activities for lengthy car trips. Share ideas of your own.

MORNING ANNOUNCEMENTS

WEEK 38

GOAL: BE A GOOD NEIGHBOR

MONDAY: Hey kids! Do you know what Citizenship means? Citizenship means that you are a member of your neighborhood. Being a member of your neighborhood means that you have an important job. YOUR job in your neighborhood is to follow the rules, make responsible choices, and be respectful to others. There are lots of things that you can do to show citizenship and to be a good neighbor. Can you think of some?

TUESDAY: Hey kids! One way to be a good neighbor is to make sure you put your garbage in the garbage can. Empty drink bottles, popsicle sticks and candy and gum wrappers should NEVER be thrown on the ground or out your car window. If you see garbage on the ground – even if it isn't yours, please take a minute to pick it up and throw it out. You show good citizenship when you do your best to keep your neighborhood clean.

WEDNESDAY: Hey kids! Being a good neighbor means doing your best to play quietly during times when your neighbors might be sleeping. Afternoon naps and earlier bedtimes can be expected for families with small children. Your good citizenship and character shines through when you do your best to be a peaceful neighbor.

THURSDAY: Hey kids! Are there children in your neighborhood who don't seem to have friends to play with? Think about inviting them to join you the next time you are playing outside. Including other children in your games is a kind thing to do in the neighborhood.

FRIDAY: Hey kids! Riding bikes and playing outside are two fun summer activities! Did you know that if you want to play in a neighbor's yard or ride your bike in their driveway, it is best to ask their permission first? Asking permission ahead of time is a good safety rule and shows respect for your neighbor.

GOAL-OF-THE-WEEK DAILY MINI-LESSONS

WEEK 38
TOPIC: BE SAFE FOR THE SUMMER
GOAL: BE A GOOD NEIGHBOR

MONDAY: Have a discussion with students about citizenship. Citizenship means being a member of and supporting one's community and country. A United States citizen has certain freedoms which are declared in the *U.S. Bill of Rights*. In addition to these privileges, a citizen has an obligation to be informed, law abiding, and uphold basic democratic principles such as tolerance and civic responsibility. Voting, conserving natural resources and taking care of oneself are all part of citizenship.

TUESDAY: Don't be a litter bug! Put drink bottles, ice cream, candy and gum wrappers in the garbage. Anything that can be recycled should go into a separate garbage container. If you come across someone else's garbage, help to keep your neighborhood clean by picking it up and putting it in it's proper place.

WEDNESDAY: Be a good neighbor by being aware of the time of day and the noise of your play. If you have a neighbor that has small children who nap and/or go to bed early, try to keep the noise level down while they are sleeping. Be considerate of those who sleep later or go to bed early by keeping the noise down early and late in the day. Keep outdoor music volumes down to avoid disturbing others.

THURSDAY: Be a good neighbor by including children who might not have anyone to play with. Consider organizing (with the help of an adult) a group of people to clean up a local park, plant flowers, collect used toys and/or clothes to be donated to those in need, visit an elderly neighbor, wash someone's car.

FRIDAY: Did you know? It is courteous to not play in or "cut" through someone else's property without permission. Use walkways and sidewalks, where available. Don't play or ride your bike in someone else's driveway/yard without permission.

MORNING ANNOUNCEMENTS

GOAL: BE SAFE FOR THE SUMMER

MONDAY: Hey kids! Do you remember the numbers to dial on the telephone if there is an emergency? If you remember, say the numbers with me. Ready? 9-1-1. Say it again with me. 9-1-1. Remember that the rule for dialing 9-1-1 is, "Only in an emergency; never as a joke." It's good to know that help will come quickly if there is an emergency and you dial 9-1-1.

TUESDAY: Hey kids! Remember that the safest place for you to ride when you are in the car is the back seat! Even when you have a very short car ride, you should be buckled in the back seat. Show your great character by remembering and following important safety rules this summer!

WEDNESDAY: Hey kids! Remember to properly secure your helmet on your head each and every time you ride a bike, scooter, skateboard, rollerblades or skates this summer! Don't ride in the road or in parking lots where drivers might not see you. Keep your head safe and have a great summer!

THURSDAY: Hey kids! Swimming sure is a fun summer activity! Make sure that you remember the important safety rule to never go in or near the water without an adult. Even if you already know how to swim, it is never safe for children to be in or around the water without a grown up. Show your good character by making safe choices around the water this summer!

FRIDAY: Hey kids! There are so many wonderfully fun things to do outside over the summer. Make sure that when you are outside, that a grown-up knows where you are at all times. Checking in with an adult shows your good safety skills and helps to make sure that a grown up will be able to find you if they need to. Show your great character by remembering and following important safety rules this summer!

GOAL-OF-THE-WEEK DAILY MINI-LESSONS

WEEK 39
TOPIC: BE SAFE FOR THE SUMMER
GOAL: BE SAFE FOR THE SUMMER

MONDAY: Ask the children if they remember the three numbers they can call on a telephone if there is an emergency? 9-1-1. Have the children (especially primary grade students) repeat the numbers several times.

Discussion should center around the types of things that constitute an emergency (and justify a 9-1-1 call): when an adult instructs you to call, when the adult in charge is gushing blood or unconscious (I explain this as suddenly falling asleep and not able to wake up), when there is a fire (remind them to exit the premise before calling), etc.

Let children know that 9-1-1 operators are there to help. They are very nice people who will send help in an emergency. Explain that the children will need to stay on the phone and answer some questions so that they are able to send the right kind of help – police, ambulance, or fire truck. I tell kids a story of a time when I called 9-1-1 when I didn't know if it was an emergency or not. The 9-1-1 operator helped me to decide what to do.

"9-1-1. Only in an emergency. Never as a joke."

TUESDAY: Review automobile passenger safety with students. Sitting in the backseat with seatbelt buckled is the safest place to ride. If they are with an adult who tells them it's okay to sit in the front, instruct them to say, "No thanks. I learned in school that it's safest for me to ride in the back."

WEDNESDAY: Review helmet safety rules with students. Tell them that the law in most areas prohibit children from riding without a helmet. Discuss reasons for having such a law. Let children know that if they don't have a helmet, they need to choose a different (non-wheel) activity. Stay away from roads and parking lots where car drivers might not see you.

THURSDAY: Swimming is such a fun summer activity. Review water safety rules with students; never go in or around the water without an adult. Even if you already know how to swim in deep water without help, you should never swim alone.

FRIDAY: It's so much fun to play outdoors and be with friends in the summer! Make sure that your grown-up knows where you are at all times. If something changes about where you will be playing, check back in with the grown-up to make sure it's okay. It's important for your safety that an adult knows where you are at all times.

MORNING ANNOUNCEMENTS

GOAL: BE SAFE FOR THE SUMMER!

MONDAY: Hey kids! Turn off those television sets and video games this summer and get outside and have some fun! The sunshine and fresh air outdoors are great for your health and well being. You can ride bikes, swing, play tag, hide-and-seek and lots of other things too! What kinds of fun things can you think of to do outside this summer?

TUESDAY: Hey kids! When you are outside this summer, make sure that you wear sunscreen so that your skin won't get sunburned. Sunburn isn't good for your skin and it sure does hurt! Wearing sunscreen will help to ensure that your time outside will be enjoyable.

WEDNESDAY: Hey kids! If you have animals at home, please make sure that they always have clean, fresh water to drink and a shady spot to rest. When the days are hot for us, you can be sure that our furry friends are hot too! Making sure that our animals always have clean, fresh water and a shady spot shows our caring and empathy, and is an important part of taking care of animals.

THURSDAY: Hey kids! Do you know something that you can do this summer to help your brain grow? Read a book!!! If you want your brain to grow even BIGGER, read another book! And if you want your brain to keep on growing all summer long, then, READ, READ, READ! Reading is a wonderful thing to do all of the days of the year…especially the summer!

FRIDAY: Hey kids! We have been talking about important things to remember to ensure that you have a safe and happy summer. Today, I want you to remember one last thing. Remember all of our important safety rules, and remember to HAVE FUN! We will be excited to see you after summer vacation is over!

GOAL-OF-THE-WEEK DAILY MINI-LESSONS

WEEK 40
TOPIC: BE SAFE FOR THE SUMMER
GOAL: BE SAFE FOR THE SUMMER

MONDAY: Talk to students about limiting the amount of "screen time" they have this summer. Outdoor activities are great for exercise and good health. Allow students to brainstorm a list of favorite summertime activities that have nothing whatsoever to do with screens!

TUESDAY: Outdoor play can result in sunburn. OUCH! Wearing sunscreen can help protect your skin from getting burned from the sun. Sunburn hurts and can make it hard for you to get a good night's sleep. If you don't have sunscreen, wearing lightweight long-sleeved shirts and pants will help protect your skin from the sun's harmful rays.

WEDNESDAY: Discuss the importance of making certain that household pets have clean, fresh water and a shady spot to rest at all times. Summer days can get quite warm for US! Think about how hot you would feel if you had your winter clothing on all day long!! Our furry friends get extremely warm during the summer months, and need our help to stay as cool and comfortable as possible.

THURSDAY: Reading is a wonderful summer activity that helps your brain to continue to grow during the days you aren't in school. The best part is that reading doesn't require other people or transportation or money. What kinds of things do YOU like to read about? Reading will help you to be your best learner when you return to school at the end of the summer.

FRIDAY: Summer is a wonderful time to run and play and laugh and grow! Remember all of the safety tips we've talked about, and have a wonderful summer!

Kim Edmister has spent her career as an elementary school counselor writing curriculum that caters to the needs of today's youth and supports proactive school-wide character education efforts. She obtained a BA in Psychology from Southern Methodist University, an MS Ed in Counseling from Alfred University, and an MA in Marriage and Family Therapy from Syracuse University. Kim is the author of "BIG DEALS and little deals...and what to do when they happen to you" -an innovative approach for teaching children how to problem solve every day problems. Kim currently lives and works in western New York, where she is regarded by her students as, "sort of, kind of, a little bit like a movie star."